GIVE ME 40 DAYS

for HEALING

GIVE ME 40 DAYS for HEALING

Freeda Bowers

Bridge-Logos

Newberry, Florida 32669 USA

Bridge Logos

Newberry, Florida 32669 USA

Give Me 40 Days for Healing
by Freeda Bowers

Copyright ©2003 by Bridge-Logos

Second edition 2007

All Rights Reserved

Printed in the United States of America

Library of Congress Catalog Card Number: 2014949111
International Standard Book Number: 978-1-61036-139-2

Dedication

To the memory of my loving natural father,

Tup McWaters, who forever remains in my heart as

invincible and a beautiful expression of Jesus in my life.

I'll love you always, Daddy.

Acknowledgements

First and foremost I give all my love, devotion and appreciation to the Holy Spirit who freely imparted to me the fullness of truth that Healing, Health and Wholeness are Finished Works of Calvary and are readily available to me.

To Dr. Larry Keefauver, for his wisdom, direction and constant encouragement.

To the countless laborers who invested their giftings and talents to make this work a reality. Without the efforts of many hands this word of wholeness could have never ascended any higher than my heart.

Endorsements

We have entered the season I have dreamed about since I was a young man. It is time for the entire Body of Christ to rise up healed and go forth in wholeness as a testimony to the world that Jesus lives. Freeda Bowers has a fresh revelation on how to release the healing virtue of Jesus to your physical body. Enjoy your **40 Day** journey to wholeness.

—Oral Roberts

God didn't intend for healing to be hard to receive! If you have the faith to be born again, you have sufficient faith for your healing. You just need to learn how to use it. This book by my friend, Freeda Bowers, reveals God's instructions on how to have healing faith and get your miracle. If you are sick or know someone who is… don't put this book down—IT'S FOR YOU!

—Marilyn Hickey

Change can happen in a moment; however, transition takes place over time. Believe it or not "40" is the symbolic number in scripture for transition. It actually takes about forty days to move through a transition in attitudes and behaviors. In every one of her books, Freeda Bowers has always had a timely and practical word on living out what God has worked into our lives. This work is equally timely, powerful, practical and compelling. I can assure you that if you will embrace the **40 Day** journey that she lays out for you, you will move into a new place of wholeness, well-being and healing. The transition will be enjoyable, I assure you!

—Dr. Mark J. Chironna

Table of Contents

Introduction

Give Me 40 Days for Healing

I pray that you will feel His glorious touch—the touch that gives everlasting life; the touch that forgives; the touch of power through which He does a mighty work in you.
—Kathryn Kuhlman

Have you ever said, "Lord, something's got to give?" Is your health, or the health of someone you love, suffering? Do you need God's healing touch in your body or mind? Are you so critically ill that you can't give of yourself to your family, friends and, most importantly, to God? If so, hold on... Don't quit... Don't give up. God is speaking to you just as He did to me. The Great Physician is very personal and wants to meet you right where you are. Even if you feel your life slipping into the grips of death, it's not too late. The Almighty God is your Healer and is present to heal you.

Congratulations on picking up this book. Hope is on the way. You have made a great choice and now have in your hands a book that can transform your life... forever! You have in your hands a **40-Day** devotional that can lead you into divine health and wholeness in your life.

Over the years, God has revealed to me that one of my primary callings in life is to bring people into His presence by delivering hope. This book shares with you the story of my first **40-Day** journey with God and is filled with many hope-filled, life-changing nuggets from scripture that can lead you into health and wholeness. Also included in this book is a devotional, but not just any devotional. The pages of this devotional are anointed by God to do a unique, exciting, transforming and healing work in your life as you spend **40 Days** with Him.

Throughout the Bible, the time period of **40 Days** had a special significance for men like Noah, Moses, Elijah and Jonah who each spent **40 Days** with God and then went on to conquer despair, win battles, overcome depression, defeat temptation and be refreshed with hope. Even Jesus Himself was led by the Holy Spirit to spend **40 Days** with God. There is clearly something significant about the number 40 and our relationship with the Lord.

God urged me to write this book just for you so that you might be healed and live a long life of divine health. God wants you to go from being sick and overwhelmed to overflowing with His presence and power in your life. I am very excited to tell you that by committing a period of **40 Days** to God, you can begin your own personal journey of hope that will take you into the presence of the Holy and Great Physician, the only One who can bring you into divine health and wholeness. Over and over again, I have seen that giving God **40 Days** has released His hand in my life and built my faith to believe Him for great things. God loves you and wants the best for you. By giving Him **40 Days** you can expect to see Him meet you at the point of your need and also witness His joy and peace as you abound in hope. My prayer for you is this:

"Now the God of hope fill you with all joy and peace in believing, that ye may abound in hope, through the power of the Holy Ghost" (Romans 15:13).

In the coming pages of **Give Me 40 Days for Healing** I will share with you...

- That spending **40 Days** with God is Biblical, life changing and overflowing with health, strength, hope and healing power
- That God will give you the strength, patience, enthusiasm and hope to spend **40 Days** with Him
- How to pray, study, listen and spend time with God daily
- What God does with your needs for healing
- That God also puts the health and wholeness needs of others in your heart
- How to willingly walk in faith and obedience as you hear God's voice for a whole and abundant life in Christ
- How to identify open doors where the enemy may have found a license to bring you sickness or disease
- How Jesus healed

> *God urged me to write this book just for you so that you might be healed and live a long life of divine health.*

On the pages ahead you will receive an invitation to give God **40 Days** to release a manifestation of healing in your body, but please don't think that it always takes **40 Days** to receive a healing. That's not true at all. There is no scriptural reference to tell us that it takes **40 Days** to receive health. Why **40 Days** instead of 2 or 21 or 100? This time is a covenant time between you and God and is an investment you will make for wholeness in every area of your life. The timing is simply a commitment of discipline. **40 Days** is the amount of time I suggest that you commit to this particular journey. In Chapter One I share with you how significant this specific number of days has been in my life.

Your healing may manifest immediately, and it is even possible that you may not receive the completeness of your healing until after your **40 Days** are over. Regardless of your circumstances, your mandate from God is to "Occupy Until He Comes." Occupy means to keep doing all you know to do. This book is a coach that will keep you moving in the right direction. If your healing manifests in the early part of your **40 Days** I encourage you to keep your commitment and complete all **40 Days**. Remember, this is an investment, not just something else you're giving a try.

I encourage you to expect a change in your circumstances today, and every single day, and stay committed to receive your total health God's way, however long that may take. I have learned that whenever I set my heart to stay in something for the long haul; it rarely takes long at all.

Once again, let me assure you that hope is on the way. No matter what symptoms you are experiencing in your body right now, God's healing power is greater than anything you feel. He promises to give you all you need and good health is a need, not a luxury.

"But my God shall supply all your need according to his riches in glory by Christ Jesus" (Philippians 4:19).

Right now you may be crying out, "Lord, something's got to give!" My friend, hope is in your hands. This **40 Day** devotional guide to healing can open your heart to hearing God's voice and seeing His healing power manifest for you. So, let's get started. God is saying to you, "**Give Me 40 Days.**"

"So teach us to number our days, that we may apply our hearts unto wisdom" (Psalm 90:12).

Freeda Bowers

Chapter 1

Lord, Something's Got to Give!

By 1984 my husband, Claud, and I had already been in full-time ministry for over six years. God had called us to build a Christian television station in Central Florida and our ministry was growing quickly. I have always enjoyed accounting and was the head bookkeeper for our ministry. Claud was, and still is, the visionary and our chief executive officer. We are humbled and honored that God has called us to serve Him as part of His "Air Force". Claud and I both know that we have been commissioned by the throne of God to take dominion over the airways, and we have willingly given our lives to do exactly that.

In 1984 the ministry had not yet acquired a computer and my job required spending countless hours entering the debits, credits and balances into the journals by hand. This was sometimes a tedious and overwhelming task for me. I had become so consumed in the busyness of doing the natural work of the ministry that I had failed to let God into the process, and I was on overload and really burnt out.

It was Labor Day weekend 1984, and I had taken the ministry ledgers home to work on in the evenings to try and catch up on the financial records. I had spent a considerable amount of time with my family over the weekend and had put aside a good bit of the work until late Monday night. I was exhausted and feverishly trying to finish everything before retiring to bed.

My mind rehearsed how tired I was and how little sleep I would get before it would be time for me to get up and go to my designated prayer time at the television station. The ministry had a Prayer Department, and every week our faithful prayer partners would come to the station at assigned times to pray for the needs of our viewers and partners and seek

God's guidance for another week of ministry. I was a member of the prayer team, and my assigned prayer time was every Tuesday morning at 8:00 a.m. Those times of prayer were so precious to me and such awesome divine appointments with the Lord that I always made it a priority to be faithful to my scheduled time.

As I contemplated setting the alarm to get up for prayer in a few short hours, I felt that I couldn't pull myself together and go on any longer. I had already spent countless hours on my ledgers, and the work was still undone. At that time I was carrying most of the accounting responsibilities of several different departments in the ministry, and the realization of my circumstances began to drown me. I felt a riptide of discouragement start to overtake me, and depression began to wash over me like a tidal wave.

It was already past midnight when I began a desperately serious conversation with the Lord. I loved God and wanted to serve Him with my whole heart, but it seemed impossible for

In all of my many hours of Bible study, I have never found argument mentioned as an acceptable form of prayer.

me to continue the way I was going. I was stretched beyond my limit, and I felt so overwhelmed with all of the responsibilities I had with my family and at the ministry. I was both physically and emotionally exhausted. I genuinely felt there was no way I could go to the television station in the morning to pray for the ministry or for all the prayer needs that had been called in by our viewers, especially when I had such a heavy workload and so many needs of my own.

With my unfinished ledgers lying before me, I began to argue with the Lord. Have you ever done that? Have you ever intended to pray, but the conversation with the Lord quickly turned from praise to petition and from adoration to argument? In all of my many hours of Bible study, I have never found argument mentioned as an acceptable form of prayer. Nonetheless, in my physical exhaustion and restlessness, arguing was exactly what I was doing. In spite of my agitation God graciously and patiently listened to me. In my mind, I reminded Him that I was only one person and couldn't do everything. I told Him there was no way I could go to prayer in the morning.

Then sweetly in my spirit I heard the Lord say, *"Prayer is more important."*

I snapped back quickly, still arguing, "But not everyone can do the books. Others can pray, but I need to work on these finances. There is no one else to do my job."

The Lord refused to debate with me. He simply whispered once again, *"Prayer is more important."* Honestly, I wasn't thrilled with what I heard Him say. In the midst of my telling the Lord how much I had to do, He asked me for more than I thought I could possibly give. I lacked the energy to pray at all, but He asked me to pray more. I had a multitude of needs, but He asked me to pray for the needs of others. I argued with Him that I needed less to do, but He gently persuaded me that what I needed was to spend more time with Him. He made it clear to me that prayer was more important

Then sweetly in my spirit I heard the Lord say, "Prayer is more important."

than my bookkeeping or balancing the budget.

Even though at that time there was no one besides me to work on the general ledger, the Lord wanted me to focus on Him, not on serving Him. Jesus desired my trust more than my trying and my abiding more than my accounting. I made a decision to go to the prayer room in the morning and to take my focus away from all my service and tasks. All of the disagreement left me as I made the commitment to go to the station to pray at my regularly scheduled time.

Once I made that decision, something supernatural happened. I genuinely heard, not just the Lord's words, but I heard His heart. I became aware that Jesus was wooing me. I knew that He was personally inviting me to come and meet with Him. I had a sweet inner witness that my decision pleased Him and that something special awaited me in the prayer room in the morning. Before I finally drifted off to sleep, it was settled in my spirit that nothing I could do for the ministry was more important than prayer.

That precept was embedded in my heart that night and remains with me even to this day. Obediently, I set my alarm and went to sleep, sweetly hearing the Lord say once again, *"Prayer is more important."*

The next morning, right on schedule, I went to prayer. With a stack of prayer requests in my hand I entered our prayer room. The room was softly lit, painted a soft blue and had blue plush carpet on the floor where we would often kneel to pray before the long altar that had been constructed for that purpose. That room was usually a very peaceful place for me, but that morning I was anything but peaceful. I had already lost the sweetness of the night before. I was physically there, but only in pure obedience because depression and fatigue had enshrouded me once again. I was really struggling not to just get in the car and go back home.

As I stood in the middle of the prayer room, I was weary in my body and once again felt the despair of my workload overtake me. I can still vividly remember taking those prayer requests and throwing them and watching them scatter across that ten-foot altar like cards wildly flung from a deck. I kicked off my shoes and stared blankly at all of the needs represented on that altar. In utter desperation I said, "Lord, something's got to give!" Immediately God spoke to my spirit and said, "**Give Me 40 Days**."

"**40 Days!**" I thought. "Lord, the needs I have You can answer in a week…." But before I had even completed that phrase, I changed it and said, "No, You can meet all of my needs in a day." Then I nearly chuckled out loud and said, "Lord, You can meet all of my needs right now. You're God!"

The Lord quickly said back to me, "Yes, Freeda, but I have to work through mankind." Then again, I heard Him softly say, "**Give Me 40 Days**."

Those words gripped my spirit and I began thinking, "This has to be God." I knew from the scriptures, that **40 Days** is a Biblical time frame, and I sensed that God was giving me something very precious and special. He had captured my heart and my attention again. The intimacy and sweetness of the night before returned, and His words bore witness to me. His gentleness motivated me to do what He asked. In the quietness of my spirit I responded, "Yes, Lord; I'll give You **40 Days**," not even questioning what that would entail.

I wish there were words to tell you about the tremendous faith that filled my heart as soon as I made that commitment. It was then that Paul's words became a reality to my heart: "But my God shall supply all your need according to his riches in glory by Christ Jesus" (Philippians 4:19). I was convinced that this invitation from the Lord was more than simply words in my spirit. I knew without a doubt that this was a moment pregnant with destiny for me, and I was filled with hope.

God brought to my remembrance that "40" is a scriptural number with profound meaning, and He erased any doubt I had concerning this revelation. I was suddenly overcome with a divine energy that literally surged through my body, and my heart overflowed with great faith. I had no idea what to expect in the next **40 Days**, but I knew that it would be something awesome. I was filled with confidence that God would meet every specific need I had at that time. Even greater than that, I had discerned one of His ways of answering prayer... by asking me to give Him a committed number of days and trusting Him to work.

In looking to the Word of God, we see that the number 40 is mentioned over 120 times. Some of these references include the following:

T was suddenly overcome with a divine energy that literally surged through my body, and my heart overflowed with great faith.

- Noah with his family and all the animals, as it rained for **40 Days** (Genesis 7)

- Moses on Mt. Sinai for **40 Days** receiving the Law (Exodus 24)

- The spies of Israel spying out the Promised Land for **40 Days** (Numbers 13)

- God strengthening Elijah for **40 Days** from one meal (I Kings 19)

- Jonah preaching repentance to Nineveh for **40 Days** (Jonah 3)

- Jesus being tempted by satan during **40 Days** in the wilderness (Matthew 4)

- Jesus being seen by His disciples for **40 Days** between His resurrection and ascension (Acts 1)

In all of the passages mentioned above, and in every other reference to the number 40 in scripture, one of two things was happening. The people involved were either in transition, or they were being put into position. Giving God **40 Days** of your life will do the same for you. It will either transition you from one place to another in Him, or put you into position to receive what He has for you. Either is wonderful to experience.

I have celebrated many **40 Day** times of prayer and praise with the Lord since that first one in 1984. In the coming pages, I want to impart to you the three most important things God taught me in those first **40 Days** because they remain with me still.

- He taught me that I can trust Him for everything and that He cannot fail.

- He taught me that prayer is a conversation, not a monologue.

- He taught me that the most effective prayer I can pray doesn't revolve around me.

As I remember that pivotal moment several years ago, I can see myself bending in joyful submission to pick up each of those prayer requests. After God spoke to me, He empowered me to intercede for each and every need. I was more than capable in Him. I felt refreshed and extremely strong both physically and spiritually. I had a renewed confidence that God was going to intervene in my life in a very special way. My faith was sky-high, and I was filled with hope.

My responsibility in the prayer room that day was not to pray for myself but to intercede for others. Although I had several pressing needs, the needs on those prayer request forms became my focus. The hour just flew by as I submitted myself to faith-filled prayer for others. I felt new freedom and faith surge up from deep within me. I knew that God was going to meet the needs of those I prayed for and bless and provide for me. I had done what He had asked me to do. I had taken the time I felt I didn't have and had drawn on strength I knew wasn't in me in order to pray for others instead of praying for myself and my needs. God was well pleased, and I was confident that He would help me with my every need.

When I walked out of that prayer room that day, I remember thinking, "I'm the same on the outside as when I walked in, but there is something very different inside my spirit." There was an excitement within me. I had begun to experience Jesus' promise: "Come unto me, all ye that labour and are heavy laden, and I will give you rest. Take my yoke upon you, and learn of me; for I am meek and lowly in heart: and ye shall find rest unto your souls. For my yoke is easy, and my burden is light" (Matthew 11:28-30).

At that time in my life, I probably had five or six specific needs that were creating great stress and pressure for me. None of them were super spiritual. None of them were life or death situations. Each need was practical and general, but very important in my life. Even though I had been totally stressed out over those needs before that day in the prayer room, once I left that place and began my **40 Days** with the Lord, it never crossed my mind to pray about them. Instead, God continually led me to pray for the needs of others.

During your **40 Days** with God, I do encourage you to lift your own needs before the Lord, but it is vital that you set times apart to get your mind off of yourself and pray for the needs of others as well. As you intercede and stand in the place of another, God will pour out His blessings upon you.

As you intercede and stand in the place of another, God will pour out His blessings upon you.

I learned more about faith and obedience in those first **40 Days** I gave to God than I had ever known before in my Christian walk. As I would follow His leading and pray for the needs of others, God met my needs. I cannot stress enough the importance of this key. Regardless of what you are facing right now, if you will pray for someone else, God will intervene for you (James 5:16).

Do you have cancer, diabetes, heart failure or another debilitating disease? Pray for someone else who has the same thing. Selflessly give your time to pray for someone else in need. If you don't know anyone suffering with the same thing you are, ask the Lord to lay someone on your heart. That's a prayer He doesn't hesitate to answer. Quickly someone will come to your mind, perhaps even a stranger. You might simply hear an unfamiliar name or see an unknown face. Just be faithful to call out that name and prophesy a release of the healing virtue to flow through his or her body. We'll look at that in more detail later. It still amazes me that God faithfully meets my needs every time He finds me faithful to stand in the gap for someone else. When someone is ill, undergirding that person in the Spirit is more important than anything I can naturally set my hands to do.

When God called me to give Him that first **40 Days** in 1984, I was already committed to Him. I was a woman of prayer and was very active in my church, but desperation was overwhelming me. Although I couldn't see it then, I was just where God wanted me that day. When I cried out to Him, "Lord, something's got to give," I was in a perfect position to hear everything He wanted to say to me because He had my complete and undivided attention. I was stretched and squeezed, and what came out of me was...

• Frustration
• Discouragement
• Anger
• Stress
• Guilt
• Feeling overwhelmed

In doing the ministry's book-keeping by hand, I could spend several hours just locating a single math-ematical error. Often, when trying to balance the books during those **40 Days**, I would be tempted to be overwhelmed again. In my thoughts I would cry out, "Lord, I just can't do this anymore." Whenever those thoughts permeated my mind, the memory of hearing God's invita-tion in that prayer room swept over me again. A supernatural surge of hope and strength would rise up once again and enable me to continue on with whatever was set before me.

God asked me for **40 Days**. I thought that would be impossible. I was already so far behind in my work. I thought that I didn't have time to complete my ledgers so where would I find time to give to God? I couldn't even conceive of giving Him one day, much less **40 Days**! Have you ever been so far behind in your responsibilities that you felt you would never catch up? That's exactly how I felt about our finan-cial books in the television ministry, but anytime I became discouraged I was quickly and sweetly reminded of the Lord's invitation, **"Give Me 40 Days."**

Throughout that entire **40 Days** I continued to fulfill all of my natural responsibilities and God sweetly assured me that He was taking care of me. There were still days that the natural things were left undone (I still haven't figured out how to pack thirty hours worth of "stuff" into a twenty-four-hour day), but God blessed me every day with patience, assurance and peace. He made even the heaviest load seem light. Stressful situations would pass by without incident. He refreshed my spirit, expanded my faith and saw to it that everything was completed in a timely fashion. That was good enough for me. Is it good enough for you as well?

One by one God provided answers to each of my needs without my cries and petitions. For the entire **40 Days** I attended to the needs of the ministry as usual and stayed focused on Him.

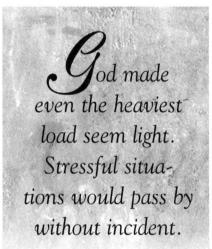

God made even the heaviest load seem light. Stressful situations would pass by without incident.

My faith was at an all time high and I was so expectant of what would happen next. It was almost as if every day was my birthday and there was a new gift waiting for me with every sunrise.

As my **40 Days** went into the second week of October, I sat back, looked at my work and realized that everything was finished! All of the ledgers were current, my quarterly reports were up to date, and I found myself with time to spare. None of my work was left undone and I had no stress. That was a miracle! The **40 Days** had passed so quickly, and I was amazed at the way God had manifested Himself to me. He is such a personal God, and He met me where I needed Him most.

I realized that I had renewed physical strength as well. That was a wonderful bonus. Although my health was not one of the things I was burdened about, God renewed my health, too. Prior to those **40 Days**, I was often chronically fatigued, but in those few short weeks I gained great physical strength. As I now look back and reflect on that time with more spiritual maturity, I realize that my mindset was an important key in helping me make it through that **40 Days**. I took the Word of God as truth and embraced it with a mindset of faith.

I want everyone to experience what I did in those first **40 Days**. At the end of that time, my life was changed, not by what I did, but by what God did in me. God's instruction in the prayer room that day has totally changed my relationship with Him. Now, in addition to being my Lord, Jesus Christ is also the dearest and most highly prized treasure in my life. He is my best friend. On the other side of that first **40 Days** with the Lord, I realized how much better I knew Him and how I could trust Him with everything in my life.

AN INVITATION TO TAKE A 40 DAY SPIRITUAL JOURNEY

I invite you to join me on a spiritual journey for the next **40 Days**. If you decide to dedicate yourself to this journey, I know that you will discover God in fresh, new and life-changing ways. He will meet your needs.

Look at your own life and answer these questions:

- Is your physical health under attack?

- Do you have an alarming diagnosis from your doctor?

- Are you facing an impossible situation in your body?

- Is sickness or pain overwhelming you, bringing fear, stress or doubt?

- Are you ready for more than healing? Are you ready to walk in God's health and wholeness every day of your life?

- Do you lack the desire to pray?

- Do you find yourself crying out, "Lord, something's got to give!"?

- Do you long for God to manifest His healing power in your life?

If you could answer yes to any of these questions, I have great news for you; the same God who faithfully met my needs during my first **40 Days**, and continually meets them to this

I want everyone to experience what I did in those first 40 Days. At the end of that time, my life was changed, not by what I did, but by what God did in me.

day, can meet yours, too. Consider committing these next **40 Days** to set your focus on your primary, ultimate and most important need, which is meeting with God, and I promise that He'll be there for you.

Take a moment right now and listen to God as He says to your spirit, "*Prayer* is *more important*. **Give Me 40 Days**." Do you hear Him?

Chapter 2

Embracing a Mindset of Faith for Divine Health

eed your faith and your doubts will starve to death.
—Abraham Lincoln

There are several different reasons to which I credit the success of the **40 Days** message in my life, but one stands out above all; I have embraced a mindset of faith. Webster's Dictionary defines a mindset as "a fixed, mental attitude formed by experience or education." I fixed my mind, not on my faith, but on the God of my faith.

Faith is the key to your healing and is an essential, vital tool in successfully submitting **40 Days** to the Lord. There is an undeniable link between faith and healing. Faith is very apparent and significant in the healing stories of the Gospel. Actually, many references to faith in the New Testament occur in relationship to Jesus healing the sick. He congratulated the people when they demonstrated faith (Luke 7:9, Luke

8:48, Luke17:19) and rebuked them when they failed to exercise it (Matt. 14:31, Matt. 16:8, Luke 9:41). Jesus was constantly on the lookout for faith and eager to reward it. It is clear that we should cultivate faith and learn to exercise it, especially in the ministry of healing.

What is faith? Faith is much more than what you believe about God. Faith is trusting Him fully. Faith always stands firm on what God says about the situation, even when the natural circumstances disagree. Faith doesn't give your emotions or natural understanding a vote. It causes you to place your full confidence in God's Word, especially when you don't know what natural step to take next. Faith can rewrite your future.

A.W. Tozer said that even though the Bible is clear about the importance of faith, outside of a brief fourteen-word description in Hebrews 11:1, nowhere does the Bible give us a definition of faith. The Bible does, however, give us numerous examples of people exercising faith. These examples inspire us and give us hope.

Many have received powerful, personal revelations on faith. One of my favorites comes from Oral Roberts who once said that faith is the power to believe what is right. That bears witness with my spirit. I have chosen to embrace the power to believe what is right. In doing that, I have put on a mindset of faith. My entire being is focused on God. Such faith builds hope and confidence, both in God and in what He will do in and through me.

I have come to know that it is more important for me to exercise faith than to know the definition of it. Like Nike says, I "Just Do It." The more I focus on God, the more I come to trust Him. When I trust Him, I unconditionally believe that He can and will do the impossible for me.

There were numerous times during my first **40 Days** that I questioned whether or not I had genuinely heard the Lord. I had to keep walking in that mindset of faith, always doing the last thing God told me to do, even when I did not yet see the fruit of it. During times that I was weary in my body and tempted to quit, faith would rise up within me and a refreshing would come as I recommitted to stand in faith and obedience. I was spiritually pregnant with a great sense of expectancy the entire **40 Days**. Even remembering it now after all these years brings back to my memory the sweetness of that time. It is as fresh now as it was then.

The Lord had personally invited me to join Him in that covenant time. Yet now, looking back, I see that I tested that voice many times during those **40 Days**. He was so gracious to me as He allowed all of my questions and patiently answered every one. God doesn't speak to me in a loud, thunderous voice. When He talks to me, it is usually so soft and gentle. I wanted to be absolutely sure that I was hearing from Him, so I asked Him many questions.

Faith is the key to your healing and is an essential, vital tool in successfully submitting 40 Days to the Lord.

When God spoke to Elijah in I Kings 19, He did not speak through the wind, earthquake or fire. He spoke through a quiet whisper: "Go forth, and stand upon the mount before the Lord. And, behold, the Lord passed by, and a great and strong wind rent the mountains, and brake in pieces the rocks before the Lord; but the Lord was not in the wind: and after the wind an earthquake; but the Lord was not in the earthquake: And after the earthquake a fire; but the Lord was not in the fire: and after the fire a still small voice" (I Kings 19:11-12).

During your **40 Days** with God, deliberately listen for His voice. He is always speaking to His children, but you must fine tune your hearing to discern how He speaks to you individually. I once heard a minister say the clearly hearing the voice of God is somewhat like listening to a radio. The radio tower transmits a signal all the time. If you turned your radio on and nothing happened, you would never think of calling the radio station to complain that something was wrong with its signal. Instead, you would check your radio. Is it plugged in? Is it turned on? Is it set on the right channel?

That's exactly how it is with God and us. He is like the radio tower always sending out the signal. We are like the radio and must be plugged in, turned on and set on the channel of what God's heart is saying to us.

Then we'll hear Him clearly every time. During your **40 Days**, find time each day to discipline yourself to silence every other voice in your life except the Lord's. Open your spiritual ears, and listen for the gentle voice of the Holy Spirit. When He speaks, write down what He says, and then quickly obey whatever He asks you to do.

During your 40 Days with God, deliberately listen for His voice.

A VOICE OF PRAISE

Faith can be expressed in many ways. During your **40 Days**, you must also decide to lift up your voice in praise to the Lord. As you dedicate yourself to give **40 Days** to God, satan will surely try to throw you off course. The best weapon against that kind of onslaught is to release your faith through praise. Let a continual flow of praise be in your mouth. The enemy may tempt you to believe that you are wasting time, especially

God's time. Just as some of those around Jesus condemned the woman for wasting expensive perfume by anointing Him (Luke 7), satan may try to accuse you of being wasteful by spending time with the Lord each day.

The enemy may tempt to draw you off course by telling you that you should be doing something far more outwardly productive, making things happen on your behalf. Ignore him. Refuse to condemn yourself for not trying to meet all of your needs in your own strength. You can't get what you're looking for on your own. If you could, you would have no need for this book, or anything else for that matter.

If you will refuse to focus on yourself, the enemy will not have a license to speak into your life .

You need a coach to get you to your next place in God, and this book can help you get there. It's no disgrace to need help. In the world of professional sports, the highest achievers have personal coaches. Even Tiger Woods, one of the greatest golfers of all time, has a personal golf coach. If you will use this book as a tool to lead you into prayer, praise and decree, you can expect Jesus to help you increase

your ability to receive from Him what He has already paid for through His shed blood.

If you will refuse to focus on yourself, the enemy will not have a license to speak into your life. Instead, fix your eyes solely on the One who meets your every need, Jesus. Do what He tells you to do, and say what He leads you to say. Just keep yourself focused on Jesus, and let your faith praise Him with all your heart. There is nothing more important than spending time with the Master.

During my first **40 Days**, I continually prayed for others and released my faith through praise. Without once praying for my own needs, they were met one at a time.

On the 39th day of that first **40 Days**, the one need I had considered to be the most important was still unresolved. I was about to give up on God ever meeting that need. I was already overwhelmed with gratitude. He had done more than I could have asked or imagined, so why be greedy, I thought. This last thing could be left undone.

But God had other plans. That very day, before lunch, He answered that last need. Isn't that just like God? He waits until you decide that He is most important of all, and then He acts. When we put God first, He responds to our needs. That's His promise: "But seek ye first the kingdom of God, and his righteousness; and all these things shall be added unto you" (Matthew 6:33).

On that 39th day, I hosted a ladies' luncheon and was so excited to share with them the awesome things God had done for me. He had answered my every specific need. Not one was left unmet, and I still had another whole day to go! Even that last difficult need on my list had been met without me struggling to solve the problem in my own strength. I was overjoyed and filled with faith. God had truly taken care of me. Hearing my testimony and the excitement in my voice moved many of the ladies at that luncheon to want to know more about having such an intimate time with God. I trust that it does the same for you.

A DIRECTION OF DIVINE ORDER

In 1986, Bobbie Jean Merck, a prophetess from Taccoa, Georgia, ministered on the West Coast of Florida, and I attended some of her services. Even though two years had passed since my first **40 Days** with God, the freshness of that time was still with me and still bearing fruit in my life.

After one meeting, Bobbie Jean and I had a meal together, and I began talking to her about the number 40. I asked her if she knew what the number 40 meant. Without hesitation Bobbie Jean looked at me intently and said, "Freeda, the number 40 means divine order applied to all earthly things and flesh."

Her words leapt in my spirit, and over the years I have embraced that revelation knowledge she imparted into my life. I have truly seen God's divine order come into numerous situations I have prayed for during **40 Days** of prayer. I also have reports from many who testify of the same thing in their own lives. I have great faith that God will release His divine order into your physical body as you give Him **40 Days** for your healing.

Don't look at the **40 Days** you will spend with God as your own time. These days are His divine time, intended to bring His divine order into your life and into the lives of those for whom you are praying. Take your eyes off yourself. Even though you will be richly blessed and reap great rewards in your life, this time is not exclusively for your benefit. Your **40 Days** are dedicated and consecrated to the Lord. This is a covenant time between you and Him. Expect Him to order your steps and direct your path as you consecrate time to spend with Him.

WHAT ARE YOU SEEKING?

Your **40 Days** with the Lord is holy. When something is holy, it is set apart and dedicated unto God. In your **40 Days**, your primary focus is to enter into His presence, trusting Him for your needs. If you will purpose to seek His face, you will not be denied: "When thou saidst, Seek ye my face; my heart said unto thee, Thy face, Lord, will I seek" (Psalm 27:8).

- Will you trust Jehovah Rapha as your Healer?

- Will you ask God how to pray for your needs?

- Will you make spending time with Him a priority?

- Will you put all of your needs at the feet of Jesus?

- Will you give God **40 Days** and trust Him with every weight and care?

- Will you seek God's face, trusting for a special new relationship with Him?

- Will you commit to pray for the needs of others?

- Will you abide in faith and be willingly obedient to His voice?

- Will you embrace a mindset of faith?

If you can answer yes to these questions you are undeniably ready to take your own personal **40 Day** journey with God. Listen as He gives you His personal invitation, "**Give Me 40 Days**."

Chapter 3

Where Does Healing Come From?

ost of us have been taught from childhood to look outside of ourselves for the answers to our problems. When we are ill we tend to look to doctors and medicine and a variety of therapies to heal us. Usually, none of those things is wrong, but I believe there is a higher and better way. The medical profession is important and often necessary, and I never counsel people not to go to the doctor. Even Jesus made reference to seeking medical help when He said, "They that be whole need not a physician, but they that are sick" (Matt. 9:12). Colossians refers to Luke as the beloved physician, so Jesus even traveled with a doctor.

I go for regular medical check-ups and will see a doctor if I have a persistent problem that I am not getting relief from, but the medical route is not my first course of action when I am ill. Running to the doctor is never my first line of defense against illness or injury. I believe that every Christian should seek Jesus first in all things and that He should surely be the first one we go to when sickness or disease attacks our physical body. After all, our body is His temple, and who has a greater interest in maintaining His property than the owner?

Where does healing come from? All healing comes from God. Whether your healing comes to you direct from the Throne in the form of a miraculous intervention, or at the hand of a physician, God is the source of that healing. He is the only giver of life, health and wholeness.

Where is God? He is everywhere, of course. He is omnipresent, but I want to focus on one place in particular where He abides. In Luke 17:21, Jesus tells us that the kingdom of God is within us. This is such an interesting passage. Jesus is speaking to the Pharisees who are unbelievers, and He tells them that the kingdom of

God is inside them. How can that be? How could the kingdom of God be inside someone who does not acknowledge Jesus as Lord?

We are spirit beings. We have a soul and we live in a physical body. Our spirit man is created in the image of God. He created us and dwells within us. All mankind has a measure of God within, but no one can access that holy thing until he or she has accepted Jesus Christ as Lord and Savior and comes through His cleansing blood.

Jesus told the Pharisees that they had full access to everything they were seeking. It was no further away than their own hearts. Sadly, they did not pursue Jesus for a way to make the kingdom and its benefits a reality in their own lives.

The kingdom of God is inside you, and in the kingdom are all things that pertain to life and Godliness. Total health for your body is in that kingdom. Your wholeness will not come from outside. It is within you. It is already inside your spirit-man, and if you have made Jesus Christ the

The words out of your mouth will be very key in your healing.

Lord of your life you have a right to access that wholeness and release it to manifest in your physical body. How do you do that?

First, of course, you must acknowledge Jesus Christ as Lord of all. You must surrender completely to Him. The word *Lord* in every language means *Boss*. Making Jesus Lord of your life begins with a head choice to accept the fact that He is the Son of God and that He died for you. Then you must willingly allow Him to be your boss. You must choose to read His Word and use it as a guide for all you do in life. Until you do that, you have no right to ask God to heal your body.

WHAT SHOULD I SAY?

The words out of your mouth will be very key in your healing. Here's a little story that will help you see that more clearly. A well-known minister I know personally tells of a time that he came to his office with the symptoms of a very serious cold. As he walked past his secretary's desk and greeted her for the day she commented on how bad he looked and said, "You have a horrible cold. You should go right back home."

The minister instantly snapped back at her and said, "I don't have a cold," and proceeded down the hall to his office.

Before he reached the door the Lord spoke to him and asked, "Why did you lie to her?" The minister was both stunned and broken. In a few short seconds the Lord spoke again and said, "You have now added lying to this infirmity."

The minister entered his office and got very still before God. "Lord," he said meekly, "I thought that I was never to acknowledge the works of darkness. I've even taught my people to only confess good things. What have I done wrong here?"

Sweetly the Lord responded and told him that the concept was correct, but the way he executed it was wrong. The minister was all ears. The Lord

spoke again and told him that the correct response in situations like that should be, "I have the symptoms of a cold, but they have no power over me."

That is a fixed law! We are not to deny the facts, but at the same time we are not to grant those facts any power over the truth of God. That minister immediately repeated what the Lord had said. He did it several times and in less than forty minutes he was completely healed.

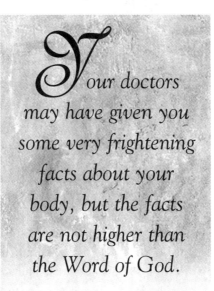

Your doctors may have given you some very frightening facts about your body, but the facts are not higher than the Word of God.

This one nugget alone is worth the price of this book. If you will begin to immediately and consistently confess out loud, "I have the symptoms of _____ but it has no power over me," I promise that you can expect a change in your health. Nothing is greater than truth. Applied truth will set you free and this nugget is truth straight from the Throne of Grace. Nothing outside of the plan of God has a higher authority than what He has already decreed.

DOCTOR'S FACTS VS. THE TRUTH

You have picked up this book hoping to find a key that will produce a manifestation of the healing power of God in your life or in the life of someone you love. Just like everyone who comes to Him in faith, Jesus will personally see to it that you are not denied.

As you come with me on your **40 Day** journey with God, I encourage you to ask the Holy Spirit to enlighten the eyes of your understanding so that you might absorb what He has for you in the devotion for each day. God's Word is so powerful that Psalms 138:2 tells us that He honors it even above His name. You are fearfully and wonderfully made by God Himself, and He does have a specific word for you that will bring the healing you need.

Your doctors may have given you some very frightening facts about your body, but the facts are not higher than the Word of God. His Word is truth and truth supercedes all facts. Knowing the truth of God and applying it to your life will set you free. The Bible says, "He sent His Word and healed them" (Psalms 107:20). That, my friend, is the truth. You are already healed. You are not the sick trying to get healed; you are the healed under attack. That must be your mindset if you are to receive wholeness in the days ahead.

Whatever has attacked your body is a lie. You must believe that and refuse to agree with the report of your doctors. They can give you facts, and you need to follow their advice while you pursue a divine intervention, but never, and I mean never, let the words of your mouth declare your own death and destruction. Refuse to agree with hopelessness. Saying things like, "my cancer, my diabetes, and my heart attack" put the power of agreement to work against you.

Proverbs 13:3, "He that keepeth his mouth keepeth his life; but he

> *Your doctors may have given you some very frightening facts about your body, but the facts are not higher than the Word of God.*

that openeth wide his lips shall have destruction."

Proverbs 15:4 (Amplified Version), "A gentle tongue (with its healing power) is a tree of life, but willful contrariness in it breaks down the spirit."

How desperately do you want to be whole? If you want it, you are going to have to work for it. Divine health is surely yours but it will not come to you automatically. It may take awhile to manifest, but healing will come to your body if you have faith in your heart and God's Word in your mouth.

To the degree that you agree with the evil reports spoken against your body you negate the power of God to intervene on your behalf. Say only what the scriptures say about your health, or say nothing at all. Remember the story of Zacharias in Luke chapter 1? Zacharias came very close to aborting the promise of God by speaking his doubt and disbelief that his barren wife would bear him a son. To prevent that, Gabriel the archangel struck him dumb for the entire term of Elisabeth's pregnancy. That's a pretty stiff penalty, but it preserved the promise.

Along those same lines of not agreeing with the doctors' reports,

I know a woman who went with a girlfriend as this friend took her newborn son to the pediatrician for his six-week check-up. The baby had been born with a serious case of spina bifida. The parents were pastors of a small community church, and the condition of this precious baby was overwhelming to them and their congregation.

As the doctor examined the baby that day, he made statements such as, "This child will never walk; he will never have bowel or bladder control; he'll be an invalid all of his life, and he will not live beyond the age of five or six."

The mother was overcome and wept quietly, but the other woman felt the Holy Ghost rise up within her and after every declaration the doctor made, she said, "That's a lie! That's a lie!" The mother was embarrassed, and after this woman had said that about three times, the doctor became very angry and asked her to leave the room.

This woman's behavior might seem rude and rather harsh, but God had divinely orchestrated her steps to be in the examining room that day, and her obedience to the prompting of the Holy Ghost brought death to the assignment of affliction on that child.

He began to heal from that very day. It wasn't an instantaneous healing, but the process began. The child grew stronger and stronger and amazed everyone, especially that pediatrician. The child was walking by the age of two; he could run and play as normal as any child. He developed normal bowel and bladder control and was not an invalid in any fashion. He grew as a healthy normal child. Rarely do children with that condition, especially as severe as this boy's was, ever know perfect health, but this story is a true testament to the truth that God heals, and all He is looking for is someone to open his or her mouth and release His healing power.

I realize that this woman's actions were radical, but sometimes you need to get radical against sickness. In case you haven't noticed, disease, crippling and death are very radical. You cannot be passive when they attack your body. If you expect the supernatural intervention of God, you're only going to get it on His terms. You must agree with His Word and speak that Word out of your mouth.

Matthew 11:12 tells us that in order to possess the things of the kingdom, we have to take them by violence. In contemporary terms, that is exactly what the woman in this story did that day in the pediatrician's office. The affliction on that baby was a lie. She simply called it what it was. You need to be aggressive when infirmity or affliction comes to steal from you. Desperate people will take desperate measures to receive what they need, and it will be important that you embrace a radical mindset if you want to see the wholeness of God manifest for you.

You need to be aggressive when infirmity or affliction comes to steal from you.

CUT OFF THE LIFE SOURCE

I am reminded of another true story. This one is about a pastor's wife who was terminally ill. Her story will give you great faith to continue believing for your healing, especially if it doesn't come quickly. This woman had been given a terminal diagnosis and was very near death. She lived with her family in Florida and was becoming more ill everyday. She believed that she heard a word from the Lord instructing her to attend a believer's convention in Tulsa, Oklahoma, and that she would be healed there, so she asked her husband to take her to Tulsa. Her husband was very concerned about her health and was reluctant at first, but he agreed to pray about it. The Lord spoke the same word to him, and he made the preparations for the trip.

Finances were not available for this couple to fly to Tulsa, so the husband began the arduous drive from Florida to Oklahoma. His wife's condition worsened on the way, and he had to stop numerous times to care for her. She nearly died the day before they reached their destination but prayer revived her, and they continued on their journey. Once in Tulsa, the pastor carried his wife to every service of the convention, most of the time having to bring her in on a stretcher. She was in and out of consciousness. One service was dedicated to healing, and they were in that particular service from beginning to end.

The convention lasted five days, and when it was over both the man and his wife were confused and stunned. She was not healed. The woman was devastated, and her husband was broken-hearted as they began the burdensome trip home. He said later that the spirit of death permeated their car and that he fought for his wife's life nearly every mile of the way back to Florida. Because of the many stops he had to make along the way, the drive home took him four full days.

Once back in Florida, the wife's condition deteriorated, but she did not want to go to the hospital and opted instead to have medical care at home. As she was able, she would ask to sit in her dining room and glance out over their backyard that had always given her such pleasure. She loved the landscaping. It brought her great peace to watch life spring forth in the myriad of plants she had so lovingly tended in her healthier days.

There was a large tree in the backyard that was diseased and not responding to treatment. One day soon after their return from Tulsa, the pastor hired a company to cut the tree down. The company that felled the tree finished the work late in the day and said they would return within the week to chop the tree up for firewood and remove the stump.

The next morning the wife was in the dining room looking out over her garden when she spotted the felled tree. The Lord spoke to her plainly and said, "Daughter, look closely at the fallen tree." She looked at it intently for several seconds, and the Lord asked her a question. He asked, "What do you see in the leaves?" She was pondering an answer when the Lord answered for her and said, "This tree is indeed dead because its life source has been cut off, but the leaves are still green."

In the next few moments the Lord spoke sweetly to this woman's heart and told her that she had truly touched the source of her healing while in Tulsa. He said that the life source of her disease had been cut off in the healing service and that the healing virtue of Jesus within her was rising from her spirit man even at that moment to drive out every remaining trace of sickness in her body. The Lord told her that all she was dealing with now was the leftover residue of the disease that remained in her cells but that the disease itself had no more life in it. He told her to watch the fallen tree and said that on the day the last leaf turned brown and fell to the ground she would receive the full manifestation of her healing.

This woman told her husband everything the Lord had said, and he immediately called the tree company and told them to leave the tree in the yard. Day by day this pastor and his wife would go together to the dining room window and watch that tree. Day by day they saw leaves turn brown and fall to the ground. Their faith soared! The life source of that tree had been cut off and the leaves had no way to revive themselves. This joyous couple watched as each leaf withered and died.

Rise up now, and in the name and authority of Jesus Christ speak death to the life source of sickness and disease in your body, and watch Him move on your behalf.

As the weeks turned into months the woman grew stronger and stronger. Daily she would go to the dining room window, look at the tree and confess over and over again, "Just as it is with that tree, the life source of sickness and disease has been cut off in my body and I am healed." In a few short weeks she was able to dismiss her medical aide and care for herself.

In due time, just exactly as the Lord had spoken, the last leaf on the tree withered and fell to the ground. That very day her body was instantly made whole. Every last trace of the disease was gone, and the parts of her body that had been ravaged by the sickness were restored to health.

Be encouraged by this woman's story. God is no respecter of persons. Rise up now, and in the name and authority of Jesus Christ speak death to the life source of sickness and disease in your body, and watch Him move on your behalf. This story took place nearly twenty years ago and to the best of my knowledge this woman is healthy and strong to this day. She took the word of the Lord as truth, and her faith never wavered. She received what the Lord had spoken to her, and with those very words she prophesied life to her own body.

"This charge I commit unto thee, son Timothy, according to the prophecies which went before on thee, that thou by them mightest war a good warfare" (I Tim. 1:18).

Chapter 4

Seeking Healing for the Right Reason

Before you begin your **40 Days** there is a question you must answer. There is no need for you to continue with this book, and quite frankly there is no need to ask God for His intervention in your situation until you have asked yourself this question and answered it correctly.

That may sound harsh, but it's the truth, and only truth can cause you to enter into all that God has for you and set you free… completely free. It is not my intent that this book gives you a band-aid for your problem, but rather I want to provide you with a permanent answer to all your health needs.

WHY DO YOU WANT TO BE HEALED?

The question you must answer is this. Why do you want to be healed? Your immediate response may be along the lines of, "I can't take the pain any longer," or "I will die soon if something doesn't change." Either of those responses, and any others like them, may sound reasonable and may be the facts, but they are not the answer God wants to hear.

There was a time that a very dear friend of mine was nearing death. She had a terminal disease and was in great pain. My assistant and I were going to the hospital to pray for this friend, and the Lord spoke to us in prayer before we went. What He said was astounding.

First, He gave us a list of things He didn't want us to pray about. That seemed quite odd at the time, but we knew this was a special moment, so we wrote down what we heard. God said, "Don't pray for the pain. Don't pray for the tumors to dissolve. Don't pray for her physicians to have wisdom. Don't pray for her immune system to activate"…and on and on. The list of don'ts was so long that by the time we were ready to leave for the hospital our entire typical "Pray for the Sick" list had been completely obliterated. We couldn't think of even one more thing to pray.

I remember it still. My assistant and I were both silent before the Lord. It was a sobering and solemn moment. The presence of the Almighty Jehovah Rapha was profoundly evident. Shortly my assistant prayed, "Lord, we have nothing left to ask You. What do You need from us today for our friend?"

The Lord responded immediately, and His answer to us is your answer to the question I said you must ask yourself. He said, "Pray that her gifts and her calling live and not die, and I will command the temple that carries them to be whole."

God's purpose for restoring health to our friend is the same for you and me and every human on the face of the earth. He longs that His plan for your life be fulfilled. In Psalm 118:17, David declared, "I shall not die, but live, and declare the works of the Lord." That is what God desires to hear from each of us. Say that out loud right now, "I will not die, but live, and declare the works of the Lord."

God desires an intimate relationship with you, and you will enter into that intimacy as you embrace His call upon your life. If you will take your eyes off of everything else but fulfilling God's purpose for your life and be faithful and consistent to confess that, you will declare His works to the world, you will soon understand God's plan for you in His kingdom. As you agree to walk in that plan, healing will rise up and overtake you.

Yes, God has a plan for your life, and His plan must be the primary reason you seek Him, especially if you seek a healing. God created you with a special purpose in mind. God created you as one-of-a-kind for something very specific, and you cannot fulfill His plan if you are sick, fatigued, stressed, weary or depressed.

> *God desires an intimate relationship with you, and you will enter into that intimacy as you embrace His call upon your life.*

The correct answer you must give the Lord when He asks why you want to be healed is this: "Lord, I want to be whole so that I might fulfill the plan You have for my life." If you will set your sights on that goal, you will place yourself firmly on the path of divine healing. Your highest form of worship is to offer your body as a living sacrifice to Jesus.

Your wholeness is not about you. It is about what you will do with the life God has given you. God is not going to heal you so you can be a healthy couch potato. You have been given an assignment in the kingdom of God, and your highest call is to complete that assignment and complete it well. Make a commitment in your heart right now to pursue your healing for the purpose of fulfilling God's plan for your life. The reason you must want a healthy body and want to live in divine wholeness is to serve the King. Let's move together toward making that a reality in your life.

Your call is calling. Answer it.

Regardless of how I feel at the moment, I endeavor to deliver hope and speak life to whomever God puts in my path.

WALKING IN GOD'S HEALTH FOR YOU

Over the years, some of satan's greatest attacks on me have been against my physical body. Often when my health was very poor, God would lay the needs of someone else on my heart. Those impressions rarely came when I had great natural strength to pray. Often, simply out of obedience I would begin to lift that person before the Lord and would perhaps give them a quick call. Time and again after I completed those calls I realized that my health was restored and I was no longer burdened with sickness. Speaking life to others brought the same life to me!

When calling those people, I was flowing in my purpose of delivering hope. I now understand that walking in my destiny puts me in position to receive life and fullness from the Father. It is so important that you know God's given purpose for your life. When you are in the center of that purpose, there is provision and protection for you that does not exist in any other place. For me, delivering hope to others is one thing that drives stress from my body and causes me to walk in health.

Over the years, I have given many **40 Day** periods to the Lord, and with each successive one my faith level has grown. I find that I am less resistant to the new things of the Spirit because the last thing God did in my life was so fruitful and brought such joy. Do you need an infusion of God's joy in your life? Is the weight of concern about your physical condition overtaking you? Perhaps during your **40 Days** with God you need to ask Him to define for you what your God-given destiny in life is. Knowing that one valuable key will give definition and purpose to your entire life.

Aside from your salvation, there is nothing greater than knowing God's purpose for your life. Walking in your purpose always draws you closer to Him.

I have now discovered that I cannot speak about or focus on the physical attacks against my body. I must refuse to walk in agreement with anything contrary to my covenant rights in Jesus. Rather, I must speak life over my flesh, pray for others and continue to walk in my purpose. Regardless of how I feel at the moment, I endeavor to deliver hope and speak life to whomever God puts in my path. Embrace this truth for yourself. It will bring wholeness to you as it does to me. I can assure you that this is a higher and better way to live.

Chapter 5

Where is the Open Door?

*S*ickness and disease can come from many sources, and we're going to take a look at some of those sources in this Chapter. I believe that finding the root cause for sickness is every bit as important as dealing with the process necessary to get well.

As we see in the story of Miriam and her rebellion against Moses in Numbers 12, sickness and disease can be the result of sin. Rebellion against authority can open a door for infirmity, and there are numerous other sins listed in the Bible that can open doors for sickness to attach itself to your body. It is not my intent here to list all of those sins. Basically, any sin you commit has the potential to ultimately result in sickness and disease. There is, however, one specific scripture reference concerning this matter that I do want to focus on because so many are guilty of this particular sin and tend to pass right by it when examining themselves for cleansing.

It's found in Ephesians 6:2-3. "Honour thy father and mother; which is the first commandment with promise; that it may be well with thee, and that thou mayest live long on the earth."

If your life is being threatened by illness, I encourage you to take a long and honest look at your relationship with your parents, whether living or dead, and also your relationship with any other person in your life that had parental authority over you as a child. Over and over again, righteously dealing with this one issue has opened a door of release for many in medically impossible circumstances. If just reading this scripture strikes a note of discomfort in you, you need to give this matter some added attention. If things are not well with you, or if your length of life is being threatened, I encourage you to "camp" on this point for a while. If you feel that you are guilty of not honoring your parents, your first course of action will be to repent. There is a big difference between acknowledging conviction and true repentance. You must truly repent.

RIGHTEOUS REPENTANCE

Feeling sorry is a quick, emotional reaction to ease the pain of guilt. Repentance is a much deeper work of the Spirit. How can you tell the difference? The Bible tells us that true repentance bears fruit. What kind of fruit? The fruit of change. In the situation we're discussing here, if there is no reversal in your actions toward your parents, or toward their memory if they are deceased, there has been no true repentance.

The Greek word for repent is *metanoia*. It literally means "to change directions, or to reverse and go in an opposite way." If there is no turning around and moving away from what was wrong in your relationship with your parents, there is no genuine repentance. You may be sorry —

If your life is being threatened by illness, I encourage you to take a long and honest look at your relationship with your parents, whether living or dead

sorry for having to pay the penalty, but being sorry is not repentance. The starting point for repentance is recognizing and confessing that your sin is against God (Psalm 51:2-4). Although others may be affected by your actions, it is against the lover of your soul that you have committed the greatest grievance.

When we sin, we plant crops of destruction in our lives. This is a fixed principle of the law of God. The wages of sin are death, but there is a secondary step we can take beyond repentance, and I rarely hear teachings about it in the church.

Proverbs 18:21 says, "Death and life are in the power of the tongue: and they that love it shall eat the fruit thereof." Look carefully at that scripture. There is such great wealth here that you might miss completely unless you allow the Holy Spirit to bring its richness to your understanding. Isn't it interesting that the first thing mentioned is death? God's patterns are always the same. He changes not. First He takes away, and then He gives. The Father required the sacrificial death of Jesus before He gave eternal life. We see the pattern of death first and then life over and over again in the Word: "...He taketh away the first, that he may establish the second" (Hebrews 10:9). "... Except a corn of wheat fall into the ground and die, it abideth alone: but if it die, it bringeth forth much fruit" (John 12:24).

When you break the law of God, that sin becomes a seed that begins producing a crop of iniquity. You sowed it, and you will surely eat the fruit of it somewhere in your future... UNLESS death comes to that seed. Yield yourself to true repentance and determine in your heart to turn from that sin. Once you have repented, in the name and authority of Jesus speak death to the crop of destruction you planted. Command that seed to die and command its life source to be cut off before it has the opportunity to bring a harvest of devastation into your life.

By the words of your mouth, you are in total control of your harvests, both for evil and for good.

By the words of your mouth, you are in total control of your harvests, both for evil and for good. Speak death and watch the fruits of destruction wither and die; speak life and you will eat life. After repentance, decree a crop failure where you have sinned and sown the wages of death.

This principle of speaking death and life works on both sides. Speak death where you want to see death. Speak life where you want to see life. Both the power of death and life are in your tongue, and with that power you can change your world.

These are the steps of repentance:

1. Confess your sin to God, acknowledging that your sin is against Him (I John 1:9, Psalm 51:2-4).

2. Forgive yourself and refuse to allow your heart to condemn you (I John 3:19-24).

3. If you have wounded someone and it is appropriate, go to him or her, ask forgiveness, and be reconciled (Matthew 5:23-24).

4. Speak death to the fruit of the crops you have sown with your sinful ways (Proverbs 18:21). The Bible tells us that we can expect to reap what we sow: "Be not deceived; God is not mocked: for whatsoever a man soweth, that shall he also reap" (Galatians 6:7).

5. Speak life where death has been present. Ask the Lord for a specific scripture that will sow life where destruction has been ruling in your life.

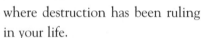

You must be willingly obedient.

After you have followed these steps ask God to give you wisdom as to what your next course of action should be. He is a personal God, and your situation is personal. In the matter of not honoring your parents, I have found that the first thing God will require is that you forgive them for whatever they did, or whatever you perceived they did that hurt you. God will help you. Just trust Him to instruct you and give you the tools you need to free yourself forever from anything that would shorten your life, or make it anything less than what He has ordained for it to be.

Sickness can also come in the form of a demonic attack, but the enemy cannot curse you without a cause (Prov. 26:2). He must have a license to attack you with sickness or disease. Looking for the open door is imperative in breaking through to wholeness and health.

Even though sin and demonic attacks are real and prevalent reasons for sickness, many times infirmity attaches itself to our bodies because of our own neglect and abuse. Our bodies have been entrusted to us for the service of God, and as we saw in chapter 4, we must take that very seriously.

DON'T NEGLECT THE NATURAL THINGS

I remember a time that the Lord spoke to me about a friend who was facing immediate and possibly life-threatening surgery. I prayed for God to heal her, but He told me that He had no avenue by which to super-naturally intervene in her situation. God is sovereign, but He has given us authority over our own lives. If we abuse that authority, He doesn't override our decisions. God honors the freewill He has given us, even if we use it to our detriment.

The Lord told me that my friend had seriously neglected and abused her health and that she had not repented of damaging His temple. Isn't that interesting? He didn't say, "Her body." He said, "My temple." The Lord said that because my friend had not repented of the neglect and abuse, He could not heal her by supernatural means. He instructed me to pray for her surgeons to have wisdom beyond their training and experience as they operated on her and that she would be healed through the surgery.

That is exactly how I prayed, and that is exactly what happened. My friend came through the surgery without incident and recovered quickly. Later, the surgeons commented on their surprise at how simple the procedure turned out to be. They had expected to be in surgery over twice as long as it actually took for them to finish. That was several years ago now, and my friend is healthy to this day.

The purpose in telling you that story is to challenge you to take an honest look at your situation. If you are suffering from a physical infirmity, you may not be in sin or under demonic attack but may simply need to repent for neglecting the temple of the Lord. If over the years you

have abused your body with things like drugs, alcohol, cigarettes, excessive sugar or anything else that God didn't intend for you to consume, you must ask His forgiveness. Obedience is better than sacrifice (I Sam. 15:22).

Obedience is necessary, and is very important, but it does not stand alone. It has a twin. You must be willingly obedient. Doing all the right things concerning the care of your body, but doing them with an unwilling heart, will produce nothing for you but weariness and disappointment.

Isaiah 1:19 says that the willing and the obedient will eat the good of the land. It takes both willingness and obedience, not just one, in order for wholeness to come to your life. If you are following a strict diet your doctor prescribed but are murmuring about every bite you take, you might as well eat a gallon of ice cream and a pound of chocolates. You'll reap the same benefits for your body. Be willing and obedient, and you will receive the goodness of God's promise of health for your body.

You may also need to repent for not doing things you should do. Things like exercising, drinking adequate amounts of water, getting sufficient rest and eating properly and in moderation. James 4:17 tells us that to him who knoweth to do good, but doeth it not, to him it is sin. We live in a society that affords us an abundance of natural knowledge on things that will help us maintain good health. Ignorance is not an excuse for not taking the best possible care of your body. God has a plan that will put you on the road to wholeness and that plan will not ignore the laws of health He has already put into effect.

Chapter 6

How Did Jesus Heal?

Growing up as children we form most of our basic behaviors by modeling the authority figures in our lives, and that modeling process continues until we die. If we have good role models, that process leads us to righteousness. If our role models are not good, our lives take a different path.

Once we become Christians, we should follow only one role model - Jesus Christ. In all we do, we should attempt to follow Him. In pursuing a healing, I believe it is important to take a look at how Jesus dealt with sickness and disease while He was on earth. What did Jesus do to get the people healed? Since Jesus is our role model, if we follow His lead we can expect to get the same results He did. Let's look at just a few of the times scripture tells us about the healing ministry of Jesus.

THE MAN WITH THE WITHERED HAND

"And **He saith** unto the man which had the withered hand, Stand forth... and **He saith** unto the man, Stretch forth thine hand. And he stretched it out: and his hand was restored whole as the other" (Mark 3: 3,5).

THE MAN SICK WITH THE PALSY

"When Jesus saw their faith, **He said** unto the sick of the palsy, Son, thy sins be forgiven thee. **I say unto thee**, Arise, and take up thy bed, and go thy way into thine house" (Mark 2:5,11).

A LEPER

"And there came a leper to him, beseeching him, and kneeling down to him, and saying unto him, If thou wilt, thou canst make me clean. And Jesus, moved with compassion, **put** forth His hand and touched him, and saith unto him, *I will, be thou clean*. And as soon *as He had spoken*, immediately the leprosy departed from him, and he was cleansed" (Mark 1: 40-42).

THE LAME MAN

"And a certain man was there, which had an infirmity thirty and eight years. When Jesus saw him lie, and knew that he had been now a long time in that case, *He saith unto him*, Wilt thou be made whole? ... *Jesus saith unto him*, Rise, take up thy bed, and walk" (John 5:5-6,8).

THE MAN BORN BLIND

"And he took the blind man by the hand, and led him out of the town; and when he had spit on his eyes, and *put His hands upon him*, he asked him if he saw aught. And he looked up, and said, I see men as trees, walking. After that *He put His hands again upon his eyes*, and made him look up: and he was restored, and saw every man clearly." (Mark 8:23-25).

PETER'S MOTHER-IN-LAW

"And he arose out of the synagogue, and entered into Simon's house. And Simon's wife's mother was taken with a great fever; and they besought him for her. And he stood over her, and *rebuked the fever;* and it left her: And immediately she arose and ministered unto them" (Luke 4:38-39).

THE WIDOW'S SON

Once we become Christians, we should follow only one role model — Jesus Christ.

"Now when he came nigh to the gate of the city, behold, there was a dead man carried out, the only son of his mother, and she was a widow: and much people of the city were with her. And when the Lord saw her, he had compassion on her, and said unto her, Weep not. And he came and touched the bier: and they that bare him stood still. *And He said*, Young man, I say unto thee, Arise. And he that was dead sat up, and began to speak. And he delivered him to his mother" (Luke 7:13-15).

There is something very significant you need to see in these verses.

Not only in these passages, but also in several other places in the Gospels, you will notice that when it was time to minister healing and wholeness, Jesus did not pray. Look over these verses again. Not one time did Jesus pray for those who were ill. In every passage where Jesus ministered to the sick, He primarily healed by one of two ways and sometimes by both. Jesus healed by speaking to the people and by laying His hands on them; He didn't pray.

I don't mean to indicate that Jesus never prayed. The scriptures are very clear that He often set Himself aside to pray to His Father and that He was in constant communion with Him, but in cases of sickness or disease there is not one time recorded where Jesus prayed at the moment of healing. That is powerful! I believe if we want to be healed, we need to follow Jesus' example. Remember, He is our role model. When it comes to healing, **you need to be doing more saying than praying.**

GET SERIOUS AND GET WHOLE

Since you have progressed this far in this book, you are obviously serious about seeking God's path of healing for you. Perhaps you are like the woman with the issue of blood who had spent all of her wealth on physicians and was none better. Perhaps you have just received a terminal diagnosis. Perhaps you are well, but are sitting beside the bedside of someone who must have the power of God manifest or death is imminent. Regardless of your situation, healing is still available for you. Nothing is impossible with God. Say that out loud right now, "Nothing is impossible with God."

I am going to make a very bold and possibly controversial statement, but one that I believe with all my heart is truth. Healing is the least of all things we can receive from Jesus... the least. Why do I say that?

Isaiah 53: 5 tells us, "But He was wounded for our transgressions; He was bruised for our iniquities: The chastisement of our peace was upon Him and with His stripes we are healed."

I Peter 2:24 recounts that same passage and says, "...by whose stripes ye were healed."

Think about it for a moment. When was Jesus beaten? He was beaten before He was taken to Calvary. If the stripes Jesus bore purchased our healing, we were healed before He went to the cross. Jesus did not have to die to make us whole. Although it is true that Jesus was slain before the foundation of the world (Rev. 13:8), in this natural realm, His death on the cross was not required to deliver unto us our covenant of health. He paid that price in full before He ever walked the first agonizing step on the Via Dolorosa.

I believe we must all learn how to attain the wholeness of our flesh, or we can abort our potential to receive the higher things God has for us. I believe that healing is the first level of our growth in Him. Are you sick or diseased? You must make a demand upon the health that the stripes of Jesus bought for you. He did not take those excruciating beatings in vain.

I am reminded that on one of my trips to Israel I visited the house of Caiaphas, the man who was high priest at the time of Jesus. I was taken to a dungeon below the house where it is believed that Jesus was bound and detained after being beaten. Our leader read from the scriptures about that place and one of the women with us began to sing,

He was wounded for my transgressions.
He was bruised for my iniquities.
Surely He bore my sorrows
And by His stripes I am healed.

Words cannot express the glorious presence of God in that place. It was tangible and so very real. I could easily receive anything from God there. Even as I remember that moment again, I can sense that same precious presence. It's right here as you read these words. Jesus has healed you. It is a finished work. Receive.

To establish wholeness in your body you must put to use the power of death and life that is already resident in your tongue. Thinking about getting well will do you very little good. You must do as Jesus did and speak to your body and command it to line up with the Word of God. Prophesy the life of God to your flesh. In the name of Jesus command your body to line up to the price of the stripes. The *Price is Right!* The stripes Jesus bore have healed you totally and forever.

You were born into this world already healed, and it is the Father's plan that you die that way. It was never the intent of God that you die

Jesus has healed you. It is a finished work. Receive.

sick. You should simply live a good life, finish the assignment given to you, and then go to sleep in Him. Anything short of that is a theft and a lie, so call it what it is, then speak death to it. After death, life must follow. Release life by speaking to your body, calling for a release of the wholeness of God that resides in your spirit-man to manifest in your physical body.

I have become intimately aware of a source of disease in my own life. In the past I would regularly open a door for stress to overtake me and allow it to destroy much of my physical wellness. Stress is a manifestation of the spirit of fear and is a killer. Stress is now recognized by the American Medical Association as an official cause of death. When stress attempts to overtake me now, I do as Jesus did and speak to the open door. In His name I rebuke the roots of fear in my life and command them to leave me.

Fear and faith are the same force; one is perverted and one is righteous. You cannot operate in both at the same time. If you are overcome by stress or any destroyer, remember the death and life principle you learned in Chapter 5 and speak to what is overtaking you. You must open your mouth and speak to it. The scripture doesn't say that the power of your thoughts contains life and death, but that the power is resident in your tongue. Learning to speak death to the source (the open door) of the sickness in your body and then speaking forth the life of Jesus to come and fill that void can become the very truth that will set you free.

Soon you will begin the devotional portion of this book. You will notice in the journal at the end of each day there is something for you to decree.

Job 22:28 says, "Thou shalt also decree a thing, and it shall be established unto thee: and the light shall shine upon thy ways."

Decreeing things out of your mouth may be foreign to you, but it is an essential part of your healing

Decreeing things out of your mouth may be foreign to you, but it is an essential part of your healing process.

process. It is with your mouth that you make a confession of salvation (Rom. 10:10). Your healing is a part of your salvation. Healing is not independent of salvation; it's just another dimension of the same thing. So why not receive the whole package?

As you read the decree for each day you may think that you are not being truthful in saying what has been written for you, but I encourage you to say exactly what is written. Each decree has been prayed over and comes straight from the heart of God. What you may be doing is, "Calling those things that aren't as though they are" (Rom. 4:17). That is an act of faith that releases the power of death and life that is in your tongue and thrusts it into the spirit realm.

Chapter 7

Instructions for Your 40 Day Journey

*H*ear, O my son, and receive my sayings; and the years of thy life shall be many.
—Proverbs 4:10

This book has been written to encourage you to begin your own **40 Days** with God specifically for the purpose of directing you into His path of health and wholeness. I believe if you will commit to give God this Biblical time period, He will meet your health needs, whether they are minor or are a matter of life and death. If you have a headache or cancer, the same Healer is present to heal you and to Him one disease or affliction is no greater than the other. I know from experience that if you will commit to this time, God will build your faith, deepen your relationship with Him, and meet you at your point of need.

I have now been in full-time ministry for over twenty-five years and have prayed for thousands of needs. When I pray for the needs of others, my personal needs continually get met as well. I encourage you to remember that your **40 Days** journey will be not only about your healing, but also more importantly about your relationship with God. As you come into intimacy with Him, you will come to realize that His greatest concern is for people. As you dedicate yourself to prayer for the needs of others, you will realize how much God delights in you and will meet your needs also.

We make a living by what we get, but we make a life by what we give away. Choose to invest a part of your **40 Days** into the life of at least one other person. Just as my needs were met the first time I gave God **40 Days**, they continue to be met every time I give Him **40 Days** and stand in the gap for others who are hurting.

Now is the time for you personally to seek God. On the following pages you will find a **40 Days** Prayer Guide.

I invite you to invest 40 minutes a day for 40 consecutive days to come into a more intimate relationship with the Lord. Before beginning, remember that you must first put on the mindset of faith.

There is a vast difference between mere belief, which is important, and belief that is connected with "intense expectation." When expectation is present, it produces a corresponding action. That is exactly what James refers to in James 2:17, when he says that faith without works is dead. You will need to put works to your faith, and as I mentioned earlier, one of the greatest works I know is to stand in the gap for someone else in need. A mindset of faith wisely prays according to God's Word and according to His promises. One of God's promises is found in James 5:16. It tells us if we will pray for the needs of others, God will meet our needs.

We always have God's full attention. One of the greatest problems we encounter in prayer is that God

As you dedicate yourself to prayer for the needs of others, you will realize how much God delights in you and will meet your needs also.

seldom has ours. It is my hope that as you take this journey you will discover how to regularly dedicate a daily time for the Lord. I left that prayer room on Labor Day morning 1984 with a seed in me that I now know was deposited to give me a lifelong desire to spend daily quality time with God. Making that a priority in my life has totally defined my destiny in Him.

During your first **40 Days** with God I recommend that you set aside 40 minutes a day for time with Him, and you don't have to do that 40 minutes all in one block of time. If you need to break it up in four, ten-minute sessions that is perfectly okay. 40 minutes isn't necessary; this isn't a formula, but it is a good amount of time to commit to begin forming a disciplined prayer life. Whatever amount of time you choose, be consistent in setting aside the same amount of time each day.

Please be conservative in your initial commitment. The enemy will come very quickly with condemnation if you make a commitment you can't keep. It is admirable to say that you'll pray two or three hours every day, but in most cases that isn't realistic. So make your commitment reasonable. God is a jealous God, and He greatly desires your devoted and undivided attention. That is what is most important during your **40 Days**. The amount of time you spend isn't as important as the quality.

REDEEM THE TIME

During your **40 Days** you don't have to stop your everyday activities. For most this will not be a sabbatical, but simply a time to commit a specific portion of each day to God. He has so wonderfully taught me to arrange my day around my prayer time, and not to arrange my prayer time around my personal agenda. If you will make your time with Him a priority, you will find that God will multiply the remainder of your day in supernatural ways. You never lose what you give to God.

In giving God **40 Days**, I have learned great lessons about redemption of time. There are many days when I have so much to do that it seems as if there is no time to give to God. Get ready. You will soon discover that the time you spend with God can redeem the time you thought you needed to accomplish the other things that need to be done in your life. I have found that if I put Him first and am faithful to commit to my prayer time, the Lord will often tell me one thing to do that may cut hours of work out of my day.

Personally, I give God the first fruits of my day. I meet with Him first thing every morning, and I think that's best but not essential. I believe if you will put God first each day, spending time with Him, He will help redeem your time, also. I have learned that if I am too busy to pray, I am too busy. *Prayer is more important.*

The pattern God has placed in my heart to recommend to you at this time is to give Him a committed amount of time each day for **40 Days**. As much as possible, the pattern you choose should be consistent. If you commit to spend 40 minutes with Him each day and complete it before 10:00 AM, do everything in your power to keep that commitment. There could be circumstances arise that would prevent you from praying at your committed time and God certainly understands that. Actually, the purpose for setting specific appointments to meet with God is more for your benefit than His, so focus on the discipline. Whenever it is in your power to do so, keep your appointments with God. There are lessons in faithfulness and discipline to be learned in your **40 Days**, and they will be wonderful tools for you in the days beyond this time.

After this Chapter you will find a **40 Days Healing Journal**. In the beginning of the journal you will find a place to list your needs for healing and a place to list the needs of others. This is a wonderful opportunity for you to see if God is true to His Word. He's up to the challenge and actually enjoys you putting His Word to the test. Anticipate hearing a specific word from God every day, but do not be discouraged if you don't. Your **40 Days** is to be a time of liberty, not a time of bondage. There are times that your spirit man will receive truth that your head is unable to receive. Just enjoy God's presence.

God longs to open up the windows of heaven on your behalf. I encourage you to heighten your expectation in God. Earnestly anticipate His response to your situation as you lift your needs before Him and commit to pray for someone else. Expectation

activates your faith. Your need doesn't move God. It's your faith and obedience that move Him.

As you list your needs, it is important that you be realistic. Reaching for an answer without wisdom is presumption, not faith, and only sets you up for disappointment. God is the God of miracles, but He is also the God of wisdom. For example, if your health problems are related to your weight, asking God to help you lose a hundred pounds in your **40 Days** isn't faith; it's presumption, and presumption never produces Godly results.

Your need doesn't move God. It's your faith and obedience that move Him.

With that kind of mindset you can probably expect to gain weight, not lose. It's much wiser to ask God to give you an easy-to-follow eating plan that will work effectively for you in a natural, healthy and productive way.

I encourage you to find a wise, supportive friend who will commit to embark upon a **40 Day** journey with you. Asking a friend to join you in your **40 Days** is a wonderful way to keep you focused. You could commit to pray for your friend's needs and that friend to pray for yours. You would be motivated to keep your friend on track because you would be expecting to benefit from the fruit of his or her prayers, and your friend would help keep you on track, too. Teaming up with a praying friend is a great way to give God **40 Days**. Together you can see amazing things manifest for both of you.

In your **40 Days** with Him you can expect to obtain the wisdom of the Lord:

"So teach us to number our days, that we may apply our hearts unto wisdom" (Psalm 90:12).

Today is the day for you to commit your time to God and allow Him to do His work in you. **40 Days** may seem too long a time for you to commit, or you may think that even if you were to pray a little, there is no way you could find time to pray for twenty, thirty, or forty minutes or more each day. Trust me - the hardest part is making the commitment. Once that is done, God will enable you to complete it.

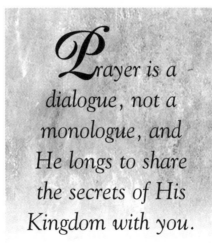

Prayer is a dialogue, not a monologue, and He longs to share the secrets of His Kingdom with you.

Let me give you some suggestions. Each **40 Day** journey is very personal and you are not bound to anything I might suggest. I am only giving you pointers on how I give God **40 Days**. Everything you do in your time with the Lord counts. You don't have to pray every minute. Begin your time with reading the devotional for the day, then you can sing, praise God from your heart, read additional scripture, meditate on a specific passage, dance before Him, pray in tongues, pray in English and if you're artistic, you can draw Him a picture. All of those things are precious to the Lord. Do be sure to pray for those you have committed to pray for during this time. You will be surprised at how quickly the time will pass.

If the Lord leads you to drop a note to, or call and encourage the one you are praying for, there may be times that you can include that time in your devotional time for the day. Of course, use wisdom. You can't spend 20 minutes talking on the phone about what's on sale at the Wal-Mart Super Center and count that as time spent with God. Giving God **40 Days** is about spending quality time with Him and for Him.

Very importantly, during your time with the Lord each day, I encourage you to give Him time to speak to you. Prayer is a dialogue, not a monologue, and He longs to share the secrets of His Kingdom with you. There is a place for you to journal what you say to God, and please, please, write down what He says to you.

Also, give God permission to work through you. Aside from asking you to pray for someone else, He may want to use you as a vessel to get something to another person. Be open to that. As the Holy Spirit leads you, be quick to respond to whatever He asks of you. James 2:20 tells us to add works to our faith. The works required of you may be as simple as picking up someone's prescriptions, taking a dog for a walk or to the vet or watering someone's garden. For a person critically ill, all of those things are monumental tasks. Whether the request seems insignificant or substantial, respond. Resist all distractions. Your willing obedience is the key during this covenant time.

Many have asked me if it is necessary to fast during this time. Truthfully, fasting never crossed my mind during my first **40 Days**, and rarely has God asked me to fast during a **40 Days** since. Fasting is a personal issue between you and God, and I do not believe you should fast unless He specifically directs you to do that. Many people have tried to add fasting to their **40 Days** and have gotten nothing more than hungry and diverted from the sweetness of this covenant time of trust. I encourage you to not add fasting unless you feel a definite call from God to do so.

I rejoice with you in great anticipation of what is to come. Enjoy your journey.

Make a promise. Before you begin, make a promise to yourself and to God that with His grace you are going to consecrate a part of every day for **40 Days** to Him, then take your commitment very seriously. Refuse to quit once you have begun. The Bible says that it is better never to make a vow to the Lord than to make one you don't keep (Ecclesiastes 5:2-5).

Commit time. Ask the Lord how much time you should commit to Him each day then set that time aside. If you let Him choose how much time you are to spend and at what time of day you are to set your appointment with Him, it will be very easy to keep that commitment.

Read Scripture. If you are critically ill, have someone read the daily scripture and devotional to you and make the decrees over you during this **40 Days**. The power of agreement is amazing. Even if you are extremely weak or unable to speak, you can make a heart agreement with your partner's words and bring about a multiplication of the power of those words in the Spirit realm. Whatever it takes, just find a way to be consistent.

Stay on course. When you do, I know you will see a significant change in your life. How can I make such a bold claim? Because there is no way that you can spend such a dedicated time with God and not experience His love and power in a greater, deeper and more personal way.

Add needs. One added thought… if a new need arises during your **40 Days**, there is no reason to start over. Just add each need as it comes. In my first **40 Days** a new need came up on the fortieth day. I just lifted that request before the Lord as if it were Day One and God answered that need before I went to bed that night. My faith was so high because of all He had done for me already that I just expected Him to take care of that need too, and He did.

This is a special covenant time that you choose to set aside to be with God, to hear His heart. It is a special time for you to seek Him and to know Him in a special way. Time is going to pass anyway, so why not give the next **40 Days** to God?

I rejoice with you in great anticipation of what is to come. Enjoy your journey.

My
40 Days
Journal

"An Investment in Wholeness"

Oh, the Possibilities!

"The wonders of God's power are to be kept alive, and made real and present, and repeated only by prayer. God is not now so evident in the world, so almighty in manifestations as of old. Not because miracles have passed away, or because God has ceased to work, but because prayer has been deprived of its simplicity, majesty, and power. God still lives, and miracles still live while God lives and acts, for miracles are God's ways of acting…. When God is seen by faith's closest, fullest eye, prayer creates a history of wonders."

—EM Bounds

Now, I invite you to join me on a special, spiritual journey that will take place over the next **40 Days**. If you will commit yourself to this journey, I know that your prayer life will never be the same. You will discover God in many ways you have never known Him before.

On the following journal pages, there are 40 scriptures—one for each day of your **40 Days**. Along with the daily scripture, you will find interactive exercises, a decree and a place to record what the Lord shares with you. If at all possible, I encourage you to do as I do and give God the first fruits of your day. That may mean getting up a little earlier than usual so you can have your prayer and Bible time before doing anything else.

I believe the Lord's Prayer in Matthew 6:9-13 shows us that the Father intends for us to meet with Him early in the day. Why do I say that? Because in this prayer Jesus teaches us to ask the Father for our daily bread. When are you going to ask the Lord to provide your food for the day? In the morning, in the beginning of the day, or as you're going to bed? Jesus also teaches us to ask Him not to lead us into temptation and deliver us from evil. How much evil do you get into while you're sound asleep at night? I believe that God wants the first fruits of our day so that He can protect and provide for us when we need it. Those aren't usually needs we have while we're sleeping.

Giving God the first of your day may be hard at first, especially if you're not a morning person, but time and again, people who commit the first fruits of their day to God discover that His grace for that day often comes in the form of miraculous interventions and the return of giving first fruits is well worth the investment. I have my devotional time in the morning, and God continues to meet me all throughout my day.

40 Days isn't a long time. It's only six weeks minus two days. So let's get started. The next **40 Days** are going to pass anyway, so why not give them to God? As you pursue Him, God will surely draw you closer to Himself and will reveal sweet and precious things to you. He will give you strength beyond your own abilities. He wants you whole. He desires to bless you

> *People who commit the first fruits of their day to God discover that His grace for that day often comes in the form of miraculous interventions.*

and use you to be a blessing to others. If you will commit to give Him a consecrated, covenant time each day for **40 Days**, I believe He will meet you right where you are. You are not too sick for the Great Physician to heal.

On the pages 70-71, write down your own needs and the needs of those that you will be lifting up in prayer during your **40 Days**. If you will look past your own needs by praying for the needs of others, you will not be denied an incredible journey with your Lord. When making your lists, I encourage you to not just arbitrarily write down what first comes to your mind, but begin with prayer, asking God what is on His heart for you right now.

If you are in pain or have a terminal diagnosis, you will automatically want to focus on that but God may have a higher plan. Yield. Allow Him to make out your prayer list. It's like a fixed race because He never gives you something to pray for that

He doesn't intend to answer. God knows you better than you know yourself, and He knows what your prayer priorities are. So often we pray out of our desperation, fear or pain, only to fill the room with empty, faithless words. Rarely, do we receive answers from those kinds of prayers. Why is that? It is because we are not praying the will of the Father: "Thy will be done in earth, as it is in heaven" (Matthew 6:10).

God answers the prayers that are for our ultimate good, not only those intended to ease the pain of a momentary crisis. He is not obligated to answer our selfish requests and is more interested in our growth than our comfort.

As you prepare your lists...

- Trust God as your Healer and source of health and wholeness.
- Ask for the Father's heart in every situation that is on your heart.
- Listen intently to every instruction of the Holy Spirit.
- Respond with willing obedience to every instruction you hear.
- Commit yourself to a mindset of faith.

- Discipline yourself to pray a specific amount of time every day for 40 consecutive days.
- Pray in a place where you will be undisturbed.
- Anticipate a glorious covenant time with your Lord.

There are journal pages provided for you each day. I encourage you to write down the following:

- Everything the Lord says to you
- Every scripture the Holy Spirit leads you to
- Every question you have of the Lord
- Every answered prayer

I have several completed journals now, and I refer to them often. Each thing the Lord gives me is priceless, and over the years I have learned that there is a greater possibility of accurately remembering those wonderful moments with Him if I have them recorded.

I am eagerly expecting wonderful things for you in the days ahead.

Let's begin.

40 Days Journal

My Needs List

_____

_____

_____

_____

_____

_____

_____

_____

_____

_____

_____

_____

40 Days Journal

The Needs of Others List

_____

_____

_____

_____

_____

_____

_____

_____

_____

_____

_____

_____

_____

Day 1

It's a Finished Work

Who his own self bare our sins in his own body on the tree, that we, being dead to sins, should live unto righteousness: by whose stripes ye were healed (1 Peter 2:24).

He sent his word, and healed them, and delivered them from their destructions (Psalm 107:20).

I love today's verses. Did you notice that both of them are written in the past tense? They make it perfectly clear that I am already healed and already delivered from all my destructions. That means my wholeness is behind me; it's not something I'm searching for now. The same is true for you.

You are not the sick looking for a healing. You are the healed under attack. If you will grasp this truth, it will cause you to take several giant steps toward a manifestation of healing in your body. Say this out loud, "I am already healed, and I refuse to settle for anything less than a full manifestation of that healing." You are already healed and you must allow this truth to settle in your heart.

If you will confess today's scriptures over and over again out of your mouth, they will begin to form an image on the inside of you. That image will begin to create in your natural body what is already a reality in the spirit realm. When God's Word takes root in your heart, it becomes greater than any sickness or disease and a manifested healing is the result.

Change your image of yourself, and begin to see yourself whole— not just temporarily healed, but completely whole. Wholeness is a covenant promise, and you are fully entitled to see it become a reality in your life.

In your journal today, make a list of any illnesses and symptoms that are attacking you. From that list make the following decree based upon the truth of Psalm 107:20:

God sent His Word and healed me. He has delivered me from all destructions. He has delivered me from _____ (and then read the list you wrote).

My Decree for Today

I am healed. I am not going to get healed; I am healed already. By the stripes of the resurrected Son of the Living God I am completely whole, and my body has to align itself with the Word of truth. I choose to set myself in agreement with the price of His stripes, and in the name of Jesus I call my manifestation of wholeness and health to be released now.

I'm whole, I'm healed,
I'm delivered, I'm free
And nothing will keep
The manifestations from me.

Only ignorance of our rights or refusal to act upon the Word can keep us ill.

—E. W. Kenyon

Day 1

It's a Finished Work

J O U R N A L

My Investment in Wholeness

_____

_____

_____

_____

_____

_____

_____

_____

_____

_____

_____

Day 2

Save Me, Lord

Heal me, O LORD, and I shall be healed; save me, and I shall be saved:
for thou art my praise (Jer. 17:14).

You have begun this **40 Day** journey trusting to see God's healing power manifest in your body, or in the body of someone you love. I set my heart in agreement with you for that goal, but I must first tell you that healing is reserved for an elite company of people. The most important thing you can do to help your healing process is make sure you are a part of that company.

To be a partaker of healing you must first be a partaker of the One from whom healing comes. Jesus Christ is the Healer. He is the only one who can heal you. To receive healing from Him you must acknowledge that Jesus is the son of God and ask Him to be the Lord of your life.

Are you saved? Do you know Jesus as Lord? If you cannot answer *yes* to both of these questions with an assurance in your heart, then you are not a part of the kingdom of God. A child of God knows with confidence that he is a part of the heavenly family. Salvation brings with it a sense of safety and security. If you cannot say with absolute confidence that you are saved, you are not a part of the company to which healing belongs. The good news is that you can join that company right now by praying a simple prayer. It is not enough that you just say the words; you must pray them from your heart. Please pray out loud:

Dear Heavenly Father,

I believe that Jesus Christ is Your Son and that He died for me. I believe that He was raised from the dead and now lives eternally with You. I believe that the sacrifice Jesus made with His death on the cross paid the Blood Price required to redeem me from all my sin. I believe that in Jesus Christ I can now be reconciled with You. I accept His priceless sacrifice.

Jesus, please come into my heart, forgive me of all my sin and be Lord of my life. In Your Name I ask these things. Amen.

If you prayed that prayer with a sincere heart, you are now a part of the family of God and are in position to receive everything Jesus died to give you. That includes wholeness for your flesh. You can continue on the rest of this journey and fully expect Jesus to manifest His healing power in you.

Congratulations and welcome to the family. If this is the first time you have asked Jesus to be the Lord of your life, I would like to hear from you. Would you please write to me at the address found in the back of this book and tell me that you have surrendered your life to Jesus?

My Decree for Today

By faith, I believe and I receive into every part of my life what Jesus has purchased for me with His own blood. I receive my salvation, my deliverance and my healing.

The greatest miracle of all is salvation. You may leave this earth with sickness in your body, but you will never enter heaven without Jesus in your heart.

—Freeda Bowers

Day 2

Save Me, Lord

J O U R N A L

My Investment in Wholeness

_____

_____

_____

_____

_____

_____

_____

_____

_____

_____

_____

_____

Day 3

Choose Life

I call heaven and earth to record this day against you, that I have set before you life and death, blessing and cursing: therefore choose life that both thou and thy seed may live: That thou mayest love the Lord thy God, and that thou mayest obey His voice, and that thou mayest cleave unto Him: for He is thy life, and the length of thy days... (Deut. 30:19-20a).

The next step you must take in this **40 Day** journey is to choose life. You must now... right this minute... set yourself in agreement with Jesus, the Giver of life, who desires that you live a long and fruitful life upon the earth. Our verses today tell us that until we make the choice to live, we can't love God. We can't obey Him. We can't cling to Him, and we cannot live a long life upon the earth.

If you are ill, you may not think that you have agreed with death, but if you are not actively putting a demand on the healing virtue of Jesus to rise up out of you and overtake your flesh, you have automatically agreed to die, and probably out of season. This is not, "Let's Make a Deal." God doesn't give you multiple choices. You only have two, live or die.

Verse 15 in this same chapter says: "See, I have set before thee this day life and good, and death and evil." When you look at it that way, this isn't real hard, is it? Good or evil? Life or death? What will your choice be? Make it now.

Meditate upon your choices as you fill in the blanks from Deut 30:19-20a:

"I call heaven and earth to record this day against you, that I have set before you _____ and _____, _____ and _____: therefore choose _____ that both thou _____ may live: That thou mayest _____ the Lord thy God, and that thou mayest _____ His voice, and that thou mayest cleave unto Him: for _____ is thy _____, and the length of thy days...."

My Decree for Today

In the power and might of Jesus Christ I choose life. I say that from this day forward, with everything in me, and with every breath I take, I put death far behind me, and I will pursue nothing but life. Dying out of season isn't an option for me. Quitting isn't an option for me. I will live and not die and declare the works of my God.

Only the man who doesn't understand the question would say no to God.

—Former President Jimmy Carter

Day 3

Choose Life

JOURNAL

My Investment in Wholeness

_____

_____

_____

_____

_____

_____

_____

_____

_____

_____

_____

Day 4

Keep God's Word in Your Heart

My son, attend to my words; incline thine ears to my sayings. Let them not depart from thine eyes; keep them in the midst of thine heart. For they are life unto those that find them, and health to all their flesh (Prov. 4: 20-22).

ealth to your flesh…. Flesh refers to your physical body. Is the health of your physical body what you're looking for? Of course it is, and here is a directive from God that will bring you a manifestation of health. God basically says, "Listen to what I say, and keep My words before your eyes and in your heart." God's words are medicine to your flesh. The Bible is His Word to you. Are you taking your God-Pills every day? To do that you must read God's Word. It is your medicine, and you must be diligent to take it. The Word know what to do.

If you are too ill to read, or have an infirmity that prevents you from reading, I encourage you to get the Bible on audiotape or have someone in your household or a healthcare provider read it to you. Actually, I think that's even better than reading it for yourself because faith comes by hearing the Word of God. When I read scripture, I often read it out loud so my natural ears can hear it, but any way you get it, you must take your spiritual medicine everyday. Jesus is the Word of God (John1:1), and He is the only provision the Father sent for your healing (Ps. 107:20).

I once heard the story of a young mother who was praying for a desperately ill child who was only growing sicker. After several days of watching her daughter suffer, the mother made a quality decision to draw near to the Lord and hear His heart concerning the matter. When the Lord spoke to her, what He said sent her reeling. She cried for hours. The Lord asked her this question, "Why don't you call upon Oprah to heal your child? You spend more time with her than you do with Me." Does that pierce your heart? It still pierces mine every time I hear it.

It isn't that God is against Oprah. He is against anything that takes the place of Him. He is a jealous God (Ex. 20:5). Where are you investing the majority of your time? If you need something supernatural, you will not find it in the natural realm. Only God has what you need.

Pay attention to the Words of God. They are life to you and health to your flesh. You are just like a computer—what goes in will come out. If you are programmed with the things of the world, that is what will come out of you. You can't expect God and His benefits to manifest on your behalf if His Word isn't in you. If you don't read your Bible, you can't receive from the Healer.

Make this commitment to the Lord today with your whole heart:

"I commit myself today to become more diligent in regularly reading God's Word."

_____

Sign and date your commitment

My Decree for Today

I choose the Word of God above all else. It is life to me and will cause the health within me to be released to my body. By His grace, I will read the Word of God daily and apply its truths. In that, my ways will be established and my healing will manifest.

You will keep your mind free from doubt and centered in peace when you keep your attention on God's Word. If you have lost your peace, get back on the Word.

—Gloria Copeland

Day 4

Keep God's Word in Your Heart

J O U R N A L

My Investment in Wholeness

_____

_____

_____

_____

_____

_____

_____

_____

_____

_____

Day 5

Forget Not All His Benefits

*Bless the Lord, O my soul; and all that is within me bless his holy name.
Bless the Lord, O my soul: and forget not all his benefits. Who forgiveth
all thine iniquities; who healeth all thy diseases (Psalm 103:1-3).*

The Word of God is sharper than any two-edged sword, and you can use today's scriptures to strike a powerful offense against anything that has come to ravage your body. The Word of God brings benefits that can release you into divine health.

The Psalmist commands his soul and all that is within him to bless the Lord. Where are you afflicted? Your heart? Your colon? Whatever it is, speak to it and command that part of your body to bless the Lord. Open your mouth and say out loud, "_____, I command you to bless the Lord. I say that this day you will rise up and bless your Creator." It may seem a little odd to talk to your liver or brain, but we've already settled the fact that you're going to have to get a little radical to see health come to your body, so just do it. Say it again and again. God releases favor to anyone (and anything) that blesses Him. Does your body need the favor of God today? Then speak to it and command it to bless the Almighty Jehovah Rapha.

When you bless Him, God grants you His benefits. Here are some of His benefits listed in Psalm 103. Put a check beside each one that you need to see manifested in your life today.

❏ Forgiveness of all my sin (vs 3)

- ❑ Healing of all my diseases (vs 3)
- ❑ Redemption from destruction (vs 4)
- ❑ To be crowned with lovingkindness (vs 4)
- ❑ To be crowned with mercy (vs 4)
- ❑ To have my mouth satisfied with good things (vs 5)
- ❑ To have my youth renewed like the eagle (vs 5)

My Decree for Today

I call all that I am, and all that is within me to bless the Lord. I say that every part of my being—spirit, soul and body—blesses the Holy One of Israel, the Great I AM. I will never forget His benefits. Jesus Christ is my healer, and I receive His healing power today.

There is nothing of heaven withheld from the one whose mouth is filled with praise for the Provider.

—Charles G. Finney

Day 5

Forget Not All His Benefits

J O U R N A L

My Investment in Wholeness

_____

_____

_____

_____

_____

_____

_____

_____

_____

_____

_____

_____

_____

_____

Day 6

Break Agreement with Sickness

Can two walk together except they be agreed? (Amos 3:3)

This verse holds what I call a "Power Punch" against sickness and disease. When I received a personal revelation on this verse I moved into a much higher dimension of victory in my life, and I know the same will be true for you.

Today's word gives us a fixed principle of the kingdom of God, and it will work for both righteousness and evil. In contemporary terms, the principle is this: if you don't agree with something, it can't hang around. If you do agree, it has the license to stay… and it will.

How does this principle apply to healing? If you refuse to agree with whatever is afflicting your body, it cannot remain. You may be thinking that you haven't agreed with the problem, but if you are battling ill health, I can assure you that somewhere you have made a wrong agreement. Sickness cannot remain in your body without an agreement with that sickness. What kind of agreement am I talking about? It could be as simple as referring to your situation as, "My heart problem." By calling the affliction yours, you have agreed with it. You may have taken your doctor's report as truth and agreed with his diagnosis.

In another aspect, you may believe that since your mother had cancer and your grandmother had cancer, you will get cancer, too. Remember, truth and facts are not the same thing.

The list of possible agreements you might have made is probably endless. Well, that's the bad news, but there's good news, too. You have the authority to break every wrong agreement you have made concerning your health. Regardless of where or how you made them, you must willingly break every agreement you have ever made with whatever is robbing your health. How do you do that? This is another one of those places where you're going to have to get a little radical. You are going to have to speak to every agreement you have made with whatever is afflicting you, and do it out loud. The enemy can't read your mind so open your mouth and speak. Your decree for today will give you a jump-start in this area.

Consider and list wrong agreements you may have made with symptoms or illnesses:

_____

_____

_____

Now consider the Word of God and list truths from the Word that you need to agree with instead:

_____

_____

_____

My Decree for Today

In the power and name of Jesus Christ I break every agreement I have ever made with _____ and I say that it can no longer walk with me. _____ you cannot remain in my body. I refuse to give you a license to stay. I will never again agree with you, and you must flee.

"Sticks and stones may break my bones, but words will never hurt me" simply isn't true. Words can definitely destroy, especially if you have spoken them against yourself.

—Charles Capps

Day 6

Break Agreement with Sickness

My Investment in Wholeness

_____

_____

_____

_____

_____

_____

_____

_____

_____

_____

_____

_____

Day 7

Appropriate Your Healing

And when he had come into the house the blind men came to him: and Jesus saith unto them, Believe ye that I am able to do this? They said unto him, Yes, Lord. Then he touched their eyes, saying, According to your faith, be it unto you (Matthew 9:28-29).

You don't have to pray for a long season to get a blessing that Jesus is eager to bestow. His compassionate heart yearns to heal you more than you have the capacity to desire it. But you can keep Him waiting if you don't have the "faith that cometh by hearing" and then act on that faith. God is never slack concerning His promises (II Pet. 3:9). He is ready right this minute to release a full manifestation of your healing. God is not making you wait. You are making Him wait.

There have been people who have prayed for a healing for many years with no results, but once they learned how to appropriate healing they received it in a moment. Your healing must be appropriated. The Word of God will be made life to your body the same way it became life to your soul, and that is by believing that there is something in it for you and reaching out to take it.

The act of appropriating is simply learning how to work with God. I like to refer to working with God as being somewhat like a game of tennis. God serves, and then it is up to you to respond. You must act on everything He puts in your court. God never cheats. He will not move out of turn. He has already given you all things that pertain to life and Godliness (II Pet. 1:3) and you have to respond to each one. As soon as you respond, the next thing you need from Him is already in position. Most of the responses God requires will come out of your mouth. When you see something in the Word that you don't act on, God waits… and waits… and waits.

These are the basic steps of appropriating your healing from God.

1. Go to the Word of God and see with your own eyes that Jesus bore all of your sickness and disease (Is. 53:5).
2. Read those scriptures out loud so your natural ear can hear them (Rom. 10:17).
3. Immediately make a head choice to acknowledge that you don't have to bear sickness and disease because Jesus bore them for you. Meditate on that. Over and over again say out loud, "I do not have to bear sickness or disease because Jesus did it for me." Don't be sloppy about this and don't procrastinate. Do it quickly and do it with confidence. If your head hasn't caught up yet, don't be concerned about it. Just call things that are not as though they are, and they will be (Rom. 4:17). Just do it.
4. Ask God to heal you. Don't beg Him. Don't be pitiful or whiney. Just ask.
5. The minute you ask, believe that you have received what you asked for (Mark 11:24).
6. Make another head choice that you are going to live in that place of receiving, regardless of your natural circumstances (Rom. 1:17). Never again waver. Be fully persuaded that God will do His part. When the ball is in His court, He always gives a perfect return.

My Decree for Today

I refuse to cast away my confidence. I believe that Jesus has healed me and I appropriate His healing virtue. It is even now manifesting in my body. I am whole, and sickness and disease is far from me.

Faith, mighty faith,
the promise sees

And looks to
God alone,

Laughs at impossibilities,
and cries,

"It Shall Be Done."

—Charles Wesley

Day 7

Appropriate Your Healing

JOURNAL

My Investment in Wholeness

_____

_____

_____

_____

_____

_____

_____

_____

_____

_____

_____

Day 8

Reach Out and Touch Him

And when the men of that place had knowledge of him, they sent out into all the country round about, and brought unto him all that were diseased; And besought him that they might touch the hem of his garment: and as many as touched him were made perfectly whole (Matt. 14:35-36).

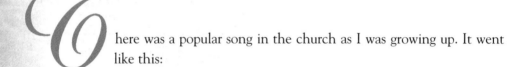

here was a popular song in the church as I was growing up. It went like this:

> *Reach out and touch the Lord as He walks by.*
> *You'll find He's not too busy to hear your heart's cry.*
> *He's passing by this moment, your need to supply.*
> *Reach out and touch the Lord as He walks by.*

Our scripture today says that all who touched Jesus were made perfectly whole. He never changes. You can reach out and touch Jesus right this minute and be made whole. Whole doesn't mean healed. It means having perfect health. I am sure that many who came to Jesus were born with missing body parts. Some perhaps had lost limbs in accidents and others had organs that had been destroyed by diseases. Yet, the Word says that everyone who touched Him was made perfectly whole.

How do you reach out and touch the Lord? I believe that's done by faith. We must believe His Word. It says if we touch Him, we will be made whole, so just choose to believe that. Don't try to figure it out. Don't make excuses why it won't work for you. Don't even rehearse the other things you've already done that haven't brought about a manifestation of your healing. Just keep your eyes on Jesus, walk on the water and believe. You may sink a little bit the first time or two you try, but if you are persistent, you will touch Him. He's waiting for that touch. Jesus is waiting to make you whole.

My Decree for Today

Wholeness is my portion, and I reach out right now by faith and take it. Jesus, I extend my entire being, spirit, soul and body to reach out and touch You today. By faith, I receive a full manifestation of all You have given to me and that includes Your health and wholeness in my life.

*If there's a way to do
it better…find it.
If you need a change
and don't look for the
better way, the only
problem lies in you.*

—Thomas Edison

Reach Out and Touch Him

J O U R N A L

My Investment in Wholeness

_____

_____

_____

_____

_____

_____

_____

_____

_____

_____

_____

_____

_____

_____

_____

Day 9

Binding and Loosing

Verily, I say unto you, Whatsoever ye shall bind on earth shall be bound in heaven, and whatsoever ye shall loose on earth shall be loosed in heaven (Matt. 18:18).

Several years ago the Lord enlightened the eyes of my understanding to today's scripture and gave me a life-changing revelation that brought a significant change in my prayer life. I want to briefly introduce you to that revelation.

Jesus was first sent to the household of Israel. In Biblical days, everyone was classified as either a Jew or non-Jew (Gentile). As a Jew ministering to the Jewish people, Jesus spoke in terms that were very common in that day. The Jews who attended to the teachings of the rabbis had been taught the writings of Moses, the author of the Pentateuch, their Holy Scriptures. In Matthew 18:18 Jesus refers to an instruction Moses had given. I believe everyone listening to Jesus the day He taught on binding and loosing understood His reference perfectly well.

Let's look together at Deuteronomy 6:6-9 to see what the Jews of that day knew that many contemporary believers have missed.

And these words, which I command thee this day, shall be in thine heart: And thou shalt teach them unto thy children, and shalt talk of them when thou sittest in thine house, and when thou walkest by the way, and when thou liest down, and when thou risest up. And thou shalt bind them for a sign upon thine hand, and they shall be as frontlets between thy eyes. And thou shalt write them on the posts of thy house, and on thy gates.

Moses taught the Israelites to bind the Word of God concerning everything that they needed to know. They were to bind the scriptures to every person and every circumstance and care in their lives. Then what would they loose? They would loose the opposite—everything not of the Father.

What a powerful key this is. I have written a booklet that expands more thoroughly on the key principles of *Binding and Loosing*. If you would like to have more information, I encourage you to get this valuable prayer tool. You will find ordering instructions in the back of this book.

According to Deut. 6:6-9, to what should we be binding ourselves?

_____

This scripture makes it clear that one way to do that is to talk of these things to others in our lives. According to this scripture, when and where should we talk of these things?

_____

_____

My Decree for Today

I bind myself, spirit, soul and body to the healing stripes Jesus bore for me, and I loose myself from every symptom of _____. Life in Christ is my portion, and His life is all I will receive.

Binding yourself and everything that concerns you to the Word of God in effect binds you to God Himself. There is no better place to be.

—Freeda Bowers

Binding and Loosing

J O U R N A L

My Investment in Wholeness

_____

_____

_____

_____

_____

_____

_____

_____

_____

_____

_____

Day 10

A Merry Heart

A merry heart doeth good like a medicine: but a broken spirit drieth the bones (Prov. 17:22).

The medical profession has long known the benefits that laughter can bring to patients with serious illnesses. Terminally ill patients are often encouraged to watch movies that make them laugh. A glad and rejoicing heart works as a medicine in the body. Today's scripture bears that out. Laughter can cause the body to produce chemicals that naturally boost the immune system. God created the human immune system so perfectly that, if it's working properly, it has the ability to fight every disease known to man.

Both Abraham and Sarah laughed when God told them that they would have a son. Genesis 17:17 tells us that Abraham was so amused at what God said that he fell on his face laughing. Could it be that their laughter healed Abraham and Sarah's aging bodies and caused life to spring up and renew their reproductive organs? I surely think that's possible.

The word *merry* in today's scripture means to rejoice. When you rejoice about something, you become exhilarated with lively and pleasurable sensations. Allow yourself to get a little extra giddy over the things that make you happy, and remember that true happiness is in the heart, not in the circumstances. Your body needs medicine right now, so give it some. I'm sure that if you're on prescription medications you don't miss a dose, so do the same with this medicine. Add laughter to your regimen. I can promise that, if you will add a merry heart to your list of prescriptions, it will be far more beneficial in bringing you to total health than any other single thing you can do.

What brings you joy? Think about that for a moment and list below three things that always make you smile.

Did you experience a sense of happiness just writing those things down? I encourage you to go over this list again and again and allow one of God's natural medicines to help your body heal.

My Decree for Today

My heart is joyful, and it releases health to my entire being. I refuse to have a broken spirit or an infirm body. I am whole in Jesus Christ, and I call that wholeness to manifest in me.

He that is of a merry heart
hath a continual feast.

—King Solomon, Proverbs 15:15

If you can laugh at it,
you can live with it.

—Unknown

There is hope for any man
who can look in a mirror and
laugh at what he sees.

—Unknown

Day 10

A Merry Heart

J O U R N A L

My Investment in Wholeness

_____

_____

_____

_____

_____

_____

_____

_____

_____

_____

_____

_____

Testimony

In 2001 I was diagnosed with stage four lymphoma and had advanced lymphoma in my body. I began taking natural treatments, and in prayer, I also took some of the treatments recommended to me by the medical profession. I had two surgeries, chemotherapy and radiation. Over the course of the next four to five years, my faith strengthened and I put my total trust in God, believing for a manifestation of His healing power to touch my body. As the Word says, I have already been healed, so I trusted God for the full manifestation of my health.

In the process of my healing my pastor gave me a copy of Freeda Bowers' book, Give Me 40 Days for Healing. It was such an encouragement to me. Freeda's teaching reaffirmed my belief that healing is a finished work of Calvary and that I didn't need to struggle for something I already possessed. As I began to read the book and meditate on the daily lessons and did the journaling, such strength came into me. I believe that Freeda's book was very instrumental in my healing process, because it provoked me to look inside myself and to really look to God and trust Him totally in the middle of everything I faced. Whatever diagnosis I was given, I was able to declare and believe that God is my healer and stand firm on His Word.

I continued to put my faith and trust in God and fully believed that His healing power and His Word is far greater than cancer. In 2005 I received a report of being totally healed and cancer free. The final authority was the Word of God that brought me through, and I am here today, a healed woman. I am grateful that God used Give Me 40 Days for Healing as one of the tools to help me face this battle with death and I give all praise to God for the healing power of Jesus and for the price He paid for me. He is forever faithful!

— CP, North Carolina

Day 11

Don't Try to Figure it Out

Be not wise in thine own eyes: fear the Lord and depart from evil. It shall be health to thy navel, and marrow to thy bones (Prov. 3:7-8).

Whenever you need an answer from God for any situation in your life, one of the best favors you can do for yourself is shut off your brain. I find that particularly true when seeking a healing. When you are ill, many voices speak into your life. Everyone you know will have an opinion about your health and the best road you should take toward recovery. Even though most people mean well, they can be used to get you off course. The loudest voice of all will probably be your body, which doesn't hesitate to let you know in no uncertain terms that it is not happy with the current set of circumstances.

Today's verse urges you to not be wise in your own eyes. The Holy Spirit is your helper, and He will lead you into all truth, but He won't compete with your natural reasoning to do so. You must give Him permission to lead you into a relationship with the Healer, Jesus Christ.

Make a heart commitment right now to let the Holy Spirit work in you, work through you and work in spite of you…and He will. He is your personal Divine Escort, and He will lead you into the safety of the fear of God and away from your own logic and reasoning. Our word for today makes it very clear that the fear of the Lord is health to you. The Holy Spirit is ready to usher you into that place.

Refuse to allow the voice of your own wisdom, or the voice of the natural wisdom of any other person, to hold credibility above the wisdom of God. Do not be wise in your own eyes, but ask God for His wisdom in every decision you make concerning your health care. The Holy Spirit will lead you to make righteous choices that can take you into wholeness.

Ask God to reveal to you any areas of your life where you may have listened to other voices above God's voice and His wisdom.

List them:

_____

_____

_____

My Decree for Today

I choose to silence my own natural reasoning and will not be wise in my own eyes. I am daily learning how to trust the Holy Spirit to lead me in all things and to teach me the fear the Lord. I know that a pure reverence of my Healer will release healing and wholeness to my flesh, and I receive that wholeness right now.

You can't keep people from having a bad opinion about your health, but you can keep them from being right about it.

—Anonymous

Give Me 40 Days for Healing

Day 11

Don't Try to Figure it Out

J O U R N A L

My Investment in Wholeness

_____

_____

_____

_____

_____

_____

_____

_____

_____

_____

Day 12

Refuse to be Condemned

There is therefore now no condemnation to them which are in Christ Jesus, who walk not after the flesh but after the Spirit (Rom. 8:1).

Condemnation is a wicked thing and is one of the enemy's primary weapons against the Body of Christ. Condemnation will cause you to take your eyes off of Jesus and bring you into defeat. You must refuse to walk in agreement with condemnation. (You may want to review Day 6 if you feel you are being swallowed up with condemnation).

As you progress on your **40 Days** you are learning sound, Biblical principles that will bring about a manifestation of healing in your body. Being taught properly and practicing these principles will release total wholeness to your physical flesh, but it takes time to develop your faith to operate in the dimension where your covenant of health resides.

If you have a life or death situation, or your doctors say you must have immediate surgery, or in other words, if your disease has a head start on your faith, my advice would be to have the surgery, or whatever else is necessary, and trust God to work through your doctors. He works through doctors everyday. If you use medical help, your position then is to trust the Lord to bring you through a quick recovery.

Most important of all, refuse to be condemned for making a decision to depend upon the medical profession. Sadly, many Christians have died believing God for a supernatural intervention when He did not have enough from them to work with. Obtaining health and wholeness is a process. You are on that journey, and

Give Me 40 Days for Healing

if you need to make medical decisions before you arrive at your final destination, do so, and refuse to be condemned about it. You are in Jesus Christ, and there is no condemnation in Him.

Until your mind is renewed to the truths of God's Word concerning divine healing, and until you have developed your faith in that Word, see your doctor, and do what he says to do. While taking medication or treatments, or undergoing surgery, continually say out of your mouth, "In Jesus' Name I believe that health and wholeness are being released out of me right now."

Continue in God's Word. Develop your faith in the healing power of that Word, and resist all condemnation. Remember to refuse to agree with anything that is contrary to what God has already said. In the days ahead you will find that you need less and less medical intervention and will experience more and more of the abundant life Jesus has promised you.

According to Romans 8:1, how much condemnation should you listen to in your life?

_____

_____

My Decree for Today

My hope is in Jesus, the Healer. He alone heals. I will pray over every decision I make concerning my health, and if I need medical intervention, I will take it without condemnation. I am in Christ Jesus and in Him there is no place for me to be condemned. I am free, I am already healed, and I refuse to walk in agreement with bondage. (In case you missed it, that's a good place to shout!)

If you follow the conviction of your heart, you owe no man an explanation.

—Charles Stanley

Day 12

Refuse to be Condemned

J O U R N A L

My Investment in Wholeness

_____

_____

_____

_____

_____

_____

_____

_____

_____

_____

_____

_____

Day 13

He Is Willing to Heal You

And behold there came a leper and worshipped him, saying, Lord, if thou wilt thou canst make me clean. And Jesus put forth his hand, and touched him saying, I will: be thou clean. And immediately his leprosy was cleansed. (Matt. 8:2-3)

Jesus is always willing to release up out of you everything that He has already deposited in you. Residing in your spirit-man is wholeness for your body. To realize a manifestation of that wholeness, you will have to put a demand on it. Jesus will meet you where you are. If you put a demand on healing, you will receive healing. If you put a demand upon health, you will receive health. If you put a demand on wholeness, you will receive wholeness. What do you want from the Lord?

The leper in today's scripture put a demand on Jesus to be cleansed of his disease. He didn't ask for anything more, and cleansing is what he received. It is implied that the leper had faith to be cleansed but wasn't sure if Jesus would be willing to help him out. Why do I think that this leper had the faith that Jesus could make him clean? Because our verse says that the first thing he did was worship Jesus.

All mankind worships something or someone, but only the Lord is worthy of our deepest adoration. You must worship Jesus if you expect Him to reach out and touch you. Our worship belongs only to Him, but we often give it away and sometimes do it so flippantly that we become blinded to the consequences. Some men will worship their sports, the stock market, their cars and boats. Some women will worship their homes, their children and shopping on the Home Shopping Network. Does any of that sound like you?

You may be giving your worship to something and not even be aware of it. How do you identify what you worship? Listen to what comes out of your mouth. The thing you talk about the most is what holds the highest place of adoration in your heart. Out of the abundance of the heart the mouth speaks.

Enjoying a manifestation of your covenant promises begins in a heart that is filled to overflowing with worship. When you yield your mouth to adore the King of kings, He enables your spirit man to release more and more of His presence to your natural man. Only His presence will change and heal you. Worship Him today.

Think back over this past year in your life, or even the past few days. Identify and write down the predominant thing you have talked about and the things you have done with your spare time:

If the main thing out of your mouth has not been about worshipping and serving the Lord, then ask Him to forgive you and to help you by His Holy Spirit to love Him with ALL of your heart and with everything that is in you.

My Decree for Today

I am a worshiper. I give all my adoration to Jesus, not for what He can do for me, but for who He is. He is my Sovereign and Almighty Lord. He is above all others. He alone is worthy of my praise. Jesus, I worship You and call you my Lord. I trust You with my whole being, spirit, soul and body. I know that You are willing to release Your wholeness up out of me and make my body as You created it to be.

Total abandonment. That's what I call it. The church calls it worship but I find that word inadequate.

—Jeanne Guyon

Day 13

He Is Willing to Heal You

J O U R N A L

My Investment in Wholeness

_____

_____

_____

_____

_____

_____

_____

_____

_____

_____

_____

Day 14

Remember the Sabbath

Remember the Sabbath day to keep it holy. Six days shall thou labour and do all thy work: but the seventh day is the Sabbath day of the Lord thy God: in it thou shalt not do any work, thou, nor thy son, nor thy daughter, thy manservant, nor thy maidservant, nor thy cattle, nor the stranger that is within thy gates. For in six days the Lord made heaven and earth, the sea, and all that in them is, and rested the seventh day; wherefore the Lord blessed the Sabbath day, and hallowed it (Ex. 20:8-11).

I find it very interesting that in reading the Ten Commandments the Lord expounded on this one commandment more than most. Four whole verses are dedicated to remembering the Sabbath. Why is more emphasis given to this commandment than any other?

You may be wondering why this commandment of the Lord is included in a devotional for healing, but I feel it is not just important, but is urgent that you understand the necessity of taking a Sabbath rest. We live in a very busy society and until our health fails us we tend to stay on the go all of the time. As long as we have the strength to go, we run like a freight train day in and day out. We fill our days with things that won't matter at all this time next year, and we neglect to give our body the rest it needs.

Several years ago, I ran into a friend who had been seriously ill. She had been sick for quite some time, but when I saw her she was beautiful and very healthy. She actually glowed with a supernatural radiance. I was stunned at the improvement she had made. I had honestly thought she would only continue to deteriorate and possibly even die an early death, but as she stood in front of me she was far from dead. She was full of life. I asked her what had happened, and she told me that the Lord has spoken to her and told her that her ill health was the result of never taking a Sabbath.

"That's it?" I thought. "You only needed to rest?" I asked her.

She assured me that all she did to completely reverse a critical illness was get serious about taking a full Sabbath's rest every week. That really impressed me, and I trust it impresses you, too. If God thought enough about giving us instructions to rest that He emphasized it more than any other commandment, we need to pay attention. Are you getting enough rest? Are you remembering to take a Sabbath?

Take a look at your calendar right now. Look back over the last three months. Or if you have been very ill, recall how your calendar was filled before you were attacked with these symptoms you are now experiencing. Count how many weeks you dedicated a day each week to a true Sabbath rest before the Lord.

Mark your calendar now for appointed times of Sabbath rest before the Lord and allow nothing to rob your rest time with Him. Make them holy days (holidays) before the Lord. It is a matter of trusting God that He'll take care of the rest of whatever concerns you. Is it the yard? He'll stretch your time. Is it the kids? Enjoy them during your time of rest. Is it work? God will take care of you. Is it worry and fear? He has everything under control. He wants your obedience, so rest in that.

My Decree for Today

I will keep the Sabbath holy and make it a priority in my life to rest before the Lord. I will honor His Word and make efforts to lighten my load so that I can get adequate rest. I commit to take better care of the Lord's temple, which is my physical body, and I trust Him to restore it and make me whole.

Our body is a well-set clock, which keeps good time, but if it be too much or indiscreetly tampered with, the alarm runs out, before the hour.

—Joseph Hall, English Bishop

Day 14

Remember the Sabbath

J O U R N A L

My Investment in Wholeness

_____

_____

_____

_____

_____

_____

_____

_____

_____

_____

_____

_____

Day 15

Your Life is in Your Mouth

Death and life are in power of the tongue and they that love it shall eat the fruit thereof (Prov. 18:21).

There is that speaketh like the piercings of a sword: but the tongue of the wise is health (Prov. 12:18).

The words you speak are vital to your health and well being. What you believe will dictate what you speak, and what you speak will affect your physical body. I am convinced by my study of God's Word and by personal experience that your words can change whatever is happening in your body. I also believe that wrong words you have spoken in the past may even be the reason you are suffering today. Today's scripture in Proverbs 18 is a reminder that both death and life are in the power of your tongue.

Science says that every system in your body responds to sound. What will you give your bodily systems to listen to? By giving God's Word a voice with your mouth, you can release a righteous sound to your body that will bring restoration and health. Fill your mouth with doubt and destruction, and you can expect to receive exactly that. There is another fixed principle of the kingdom of God that says you will have whatever you say. Jesus said that you can have what you say, so why are you saying what you have? Are you saying things like, "I am so weak"? Instead say, "When I am weak, He is strong."

I would not be amazed to discover that there are diseases that will never be healed until we learn how to speak the language of wholeness that the body understands. God's Word spoken out of your mouth is a language your body knows well, and speaking it regularly can make you truly whole. Guard your tongue so that the words you speak are always words of truth and faith and not words of doubt and unbelief.

List the wrong confessions you have been speaking:

_____

_____

_____

Now list words of truth from the Word of God to change your confession:

_____

_____

_____

Make these words from the Lord your daily confession!

My Decree for Today

I will only permit my mouth to speak life, and I forbid it to speak death. I will declare the righteous works of God and refuse to allow my mouth to agree with the workings of destruction. I seek the wisdom of God, and I choose to say only what He says. He is the Giver of life, and I choose to receive His gift of life and nothing else.

Until your spirit and words agree there is no place for a release of God's wholeness to your body. Command your spirit and words to get on the same page. Any page in the Bible will do.

—Freeda Bowers

Day 15

Your Life is in Your Mouth

J O U R N A L

My Investment in Wholeness

Day 16

Settle All Doubts

God is not a man that he should lie, neither the son of man that he should repent. Hath he said and shall he not do it, or hath he spoken and shall he not make it good? (Num. 23:19).

What God says He means, and He puts all of the power of heaven behind His Words. You can anchor your faith in what God has to say about your health and wholeness, but before you can drop that anchor, you must get rid of all uncertainty concerning His will to heal you. Accessing the faith that will release the wholeness already residing within you cannot go beyond your knowledge that God wants you whole. You must settle in your heart the truth the Bible plainly teaches that it is as much God's will to heal your body as it is to save your soul. We were born into this world under a double curse: sin and sickness. And by faith we must accept the double cure: forgiveness and healing. They come as a package. The same salvation that saved you gives you the right to access the health within your spirit man.

Jesus said that the Word of God is the seed of divine life. That seed resides in your spirit man, but until it is transplanted to your understanding, you will continually try in vain to reap a harvest from a fallow field. Where nothing is planted, nothing can come up. Until you are convinced from God's Word that it is His full plan and purpose to heal you, you will continually be tossed about by doubt and unbelief.

When you are occupied with your symptoms, you have the wrong seed for your harvest. It is impossible to sow tares and reap wheat. Your symptoms may point you to death, but the Word of God points you to life, and you cannot go in both directions at the same time, so choose life. Once you step in that direction, refuse to waver because a double-minded man is unstable in all his ways (James 1:8).

To settle once and for all that it is God's will to heal you and bring you to wholeness, you must transplant a seed of life from your spirit man to your mind and heart. You do that by reading God's Word concerning healing. If you don't know God's Word concerning healing, you must study scriptures about healing and meditate on them until they are life to you. I recommend that you start with the book of John and ask the Holy Spirit to illumine the scriptures to you as you read.

Make a list here of the promises in God's Word that you want desperately to believe, but are struggling with:

_____

_____

_____

My Decree for Today

I choose the path of life and will never again doubt that it is God's will to heal me. I accept the double cure Jesus bought for me, and I choose to walk in health and wholeness in Him. I know that my healing is a finished work, and I won't ever question that again. I will forever say, "To God be the Glory, Great Things He Has Done!

It is our unbelief that impedes the miraculous power of the Lord and holds Him back from healing as He did in the Bible.

—Andrew Murray

Day 16

Settle All Doubts

JOURNAL

My Investment in Wholeness

_____

_____

_____

_____

_____

_____

_____

_____

_____

_____

_____

Day 17

The Love Factor

...that the world may know that Thou hast sent me, and hast loved them as Thou hast loved me. (John 17:23b)

In pursuing a healing, we tend to put an emphasis on the power of God to heal. That's not entirely wrong, but it's not the complete picture. Clearly it is God's power that heals, but what is that power? God's power is His love. Actually, His power is His very being. It is God Himself. I John 4:8 tells us that God is love. His power and His love are equal; one is not subordinate to the other. I think we need to readjust our thinking and see God's love first if we are to receive anything from Him—especially a healing.

Our verse today tells you exactly how much the Father loves you. He loves you as much as He loves Jesus. Once you ask the Holy Spirit to help you comprehend God's great love for you, that love will begin to envelop you and take you up into a place where you trust Him fully. There you know that He has already made a way of escape for you. A wonderful thing begins to happen. You no longer view your healing as something that has to be done, but rather you know without a doubt that it is something already finished. You know without doubt or questioning that healing is yours. You just have to access it.

In very simple terms, it's somewhat like having a craving for a McDonald's hamburger. You know if you can just get to McDonald's you will positively be able to get that hamburger. You would never think, even for a single moment, that McDonald's wouldn't have hamburgers. Of course they have hamburgers. They always have hamburgers. It's the same with God. He always has your covenant provisions. You just have to access them. They are each a part of God's love.

Accept by faith God's unconditional love for you. Nothing will ever separate you from that love (Rom. 8:39). Because of that love the Father will not withhold anything from you that He has given to Jesus, and He has given Jesus all things that pertain to life, wholeness and Godliness.

Healing is essential to the Gospel message. If we truly believe that God is love and that He loves us as much as He loves Jesus, it then becomes easy for us to believe that healing is an ordinary, not an extraordinary sign of His compassion. Was Jesus ever sick a day in His life? Of course not. The same reality is available for us. We must simply believe it, access it and release it.

I once heard the story of a young boy who was critically ill and at the point of death. The family called for a minister to come and pray for him. As the minister went to the boy's room to pray, the family sat around the kitchen table waiting. The minister walked over to the boy, leaned over him without touching him and said only three words, "God loves you." Immediately the boy got up and ran around the room and into the kitchen. He was totally healed. He had surely caught a revelation of the matchless love of God, and it healed him instantly.

I believe to readjust our thinking concerning healing, we need to see God as love. Ask the Holy Spirit right now to cause the eyes of your understanding to behold love… to behold God. He longs to reveal Himself to you.

List two ways in which God has already revealed His Love to you:

_____

_____

My Decree for Today

I choose to believe that the Father loves me as much as He loves Jesus and that He wants me healed and whole. I put my faith in God's Word that promises me health and length of days. I will not resist God's love but will gratefully receive all He has for me.

The love of God is the most powerful of all means of health and long life.

—John Wesley

Day 17

The Love Factor

J O U R N A L

My Investment in Wholeness

_____

_____

_____

_____

_____

_____

_____

_____

_____

_____

_____

_____

Day 18

Be Thankful

In everything give thanks: for this is the will of God concerning you
(I Thess. 5:18).

It may seem difficult for you to be thankful right now, and it may seem totally impossible to give thanks to God for your illness, but that is exactly what today's verse says you must do. We are to give thanks in everything, including the difficult times. Why would God expect you to be grateful for infirmity? Is He a sadist who rejoices over your sickness? Of course not.

Psalm 100:4 tells us that we enter into His gates with thanksgiving. That means that the starting place for you to commune with your benevolent and loving Creator is to thank Him for everything that concerns you. God wants your gratitude because He knows that thanksgiving opens the gates of the spiritual realm. It is only from that place that you can obtain wholeness, and all God wants for you is wholeness. Your spirit-man must make a spirit-to-Spirit connection in order for you to see a manifestation of wholeness in your physical body, and thanksgiving begins that process.

How do you become thankful for sickness and disease? You begin by thanking God for His plan and purpose in it. God has something wonderful for you. All of His plans for you are for goodness and hope, so thank Him for His plan in this trial you are facing. Make a head choice to obey today's scripture and just do it. Don't think about it. Just do it. Begin by expressing out of your mouth your thanks to the Lord for specific things. Start with the easy things. Thank God below for five specific things in your life.

Once you get five written down, I'm sure others will easily come to mind. Just say the new ones too, and then add whatever is attacking your body. There is tremendous power in thanksgiving, and you must practice this tool often. Being forever thankful for all things must become a lifestyle for a truly committed Christian. Thanksgiving is not something you express occasionally, but it is something you become. Gratitude is the outflow of a heart that truly and fully trusts God in all things. The more you express your gratitude out of your mouth, the greater your faith will build to see a change in your physical circumstances. Give God thanks today with a grateful heart.

My Decree for Today

It is good to give thanks unto the Lord, and I choose to have a grateful heart and thank Him in all things. With my heart I praise You, Lord, and I bless Your name. You are only good. All You have for me is life and wholeness, and I thank You for the health You have already given me. I receive it now fully manifested in my body.

If He declares that we are healed, then our part is to thank Him for the work He has already accomplished.

—E.W. Kenyon

Day 18

Be Thankful

J O U R N A L

My Investment in Wholeness

_____

_____

_____

_____

_____

_____

_____

_____

_____

_____

_____

_____

Day 19

Get Your Prayer Strategy Right

According to His Divine power hath given unto us all things that pertain unto life and Godliness, through the knowledge of Him that hath called us to glory and virtue: Whereby are given unto us exceeding great and precious promises: that by these ye might be partakers of the Divine nature…(2 Pet. 1:3-4).

Prayer is a vital part of your **40 Days** with God. You are petitioning Him during this time for many things and desire answers, both for yourself and for others. It is important that you get your prayer strategy right.

Your prayers are in trouble when you don't pray according to God's rules, and He is very specific about how you should come to Him. God does not want to hear about your problem. He knows about your problem. All He wants is for you to come to Him with what He has already said about it. The most powerful words out of your mouth are, "It is written." Satan trembles when he hears those words and God reacts like a proud father as they come to His ears. You must learn how to pray properly and that means always praying from the positive side of the curve.

Do you always see the negative side of things? If you do, that is exactly how you'll go to God with your needs, and He is not the Chief Executive of the Complaint Department. There is no complaint department in heaven, so where do you suppose those kinds of prayers go? They go right to the ears of the powers in the dark realm that use the words out of your own mouth as weapons against you.

The words of your confession are very vital to prayer. Your words will either bind you to your problem or release you from it. Your health is the problem you are concerned about today, and God will let you keep it if you want it. You are the only one who can determine the outcome of the attack against your body, and you will determine it by the words you speak, both to God and to others.

Today's scripture says that you have already been given great and precious promises that enable you to partake of the very nature of God. You can release God's nature through the words of your mouth, or you can talk about your problem, pray about your problem and worry about your problem. If you do that, your problem will become greater and greater. You will become sicker and sicker, and all of the things that have been given to you for life and Godliness will remain dormant in your life.

If you talk about your problem to your friends and family, they'll believe you have a problem and talk about it among themselves. They'll talk about it to others, and soon you'll have a multitude of people agreeing with your problem.

The Word of God sets forth a fixed law of the Spirit that says, "If any two of you shall agree on earth touching anything…" (Matt. 18:19). Fixed laws work regardless of who uses them. A wicked man can prosper by using the biblical principles concerning his finances, and you can go all the way to your grave by agreeing with someone else that you have sickness in your body.

So get your prayers lined up with God's rules, and step on over into a release of divine healing. From this day forward, as far as your mouth is concerned, you don't have a problem; you have an answer. You have the divine nature of God, and there is no sickness in Him. Speak that out of your mouth.

My Decree for Today

My heart is in alignment with God's Word, and what He says concerning my health is all that I will accept and all that I will speak. The fact may be that I am battling _____, but the truth is, I am healed by the stripes of Jesus and those stripes are releasing wholeness to me right now.

You can supernaturally safeguard your good health and promote healing when you speak forth the Word of God. Put the proven power of God's Word to work on your behalf... Today!

—Marilyn Hickey

Day 19

Get Your Prayer Strategy Right

J O U R N A L

My Investment in Wholeness

_____

_____

_____

_____

_____

_____

_____

_____

_____

_____

_____

Day 20

Little by Little

By little and little I will drive them out from before thee, until thou be increased, and inherit the land. (Ex 23:30)

Congratulations! Today marks the halfway point of your **40 Day** journey. How are you doing? Have you begun to experience the healing power of God in your body? I trust that's the case, and for many a full manifestation of healing will have occurred by now. If that hasn't happened for you, I want you to reread today's verse.

God often works little by little. You may tend to disagree with His timing, especially if you are in pain, but you can fully trust the Lord. He is not slow to heal you because the job's too big for Him, or because He's busy healing several other sick people in line in front of you, but because He truly does know what is best for you. In some cases, if God moved too quickly, the outcome would not be a blessing to you.

Refuse to even think that God is holding out on you. There is no truth in that. God is not withholding a manifestation of your healing. He is waiting on you to access it. God wants you to inherit your covenant promise of health. Actually, He wants it more than you do. Remember, He has invested much into your life and is looking for a return on His investment. He is helping you as much and as quickly as you will allow Him.

You can rest in this: "Being confident of this very thing, that He which hath begun a good work in you will perform it until the day of Jesus Christ" (Phil. 1:6).

Give Me 40 Days for Healing

If you are still experiencing the symptoms of illness, right now the Holy Spirit is encouraging you and strengthening you to continue on toward your healing. What God has started in your body, He will finish. Remember, healing is yours already. Trust the timing of its manifestation to God. After all, your Heavenly Father *really does know best!*

We are now halfway through our **40 Days**. List here all improvements in your health (even minor ones) that you have seen since the beginning of these **40 Days** with the Lord:

_____

_____

Praise God for them!

If you have seen no physical manifestations of healing yet, determine to continue to trust God and wait upon the Lord! Do not get discouraged and do not fear.

My Decree for Today

I choose to wait patiently for a full manifestation of my healing. God has a perfect plan for me, and I will wait for it. I trust Him fully with everything that concerns me. I make a choice to stand in unwavering faith until wholeness comes, even if it is released to me little by little.

ready, not when God's good and ready. He's always ready.

—Oral Roberts

Day 20

Little by Little

J O U R N A L

My Investment in Wholeness

Testimony

working age man in my church suffered a stroke that robbed him of understandable speech and mobility on one side of his body. His speech was starting to recover when I began my **40 Days**. I prayed for a full recovery. I had great faith for that because God had manifested a same type of recovery for my wife's father.

At the end of my **40 Days** this man began to walk with a spring in his gait, and his speech was clear and understandable. And one more thing, he had renewed strength in his grip. This man is now back at his job working full-time. There is still a way to go to full recovery, but he's receiving regular prayer and progressing.

I give Jesus all the praise and all the glory.

—JCD, Florida

Day 21

Can I Fix It?

Be not deceived, God is not mocked, for whatsoever a man soweth, that shall he also reap (Gal. 6:7).

Do you remember the story in Chapter 5 about my friend who had neglected her body? When it came time for surgery, the Lord didn't have what He needed to intervene supernaturally on her behalf because she had not repented of violating the laws of nature and neglecting her health. Is that your case, too? Your physical body is the temple of the Lord (1 Cor. 6:19) and He has entrusted its care to you. Have you done a good job with it? If you have neglected or abused your body, you have sinned. So what can you do now? Can you fix it? Thankfully, yes, you can.

When you break the law of God, that sin becomes a seed that begins creating a harvest. You sowed that seed, and you will surely eat the fruit of it somewhere in your future... UNLESS death comes to that seed. The only way you can bring death to seeds of destruction you have sown is by first yielding yourself to true repentance. You must ask God's forgiveness, and you must also stop doing what brought you to where you are now.

True repentance requires a change in behavior. Once you have repented, you can then rise up in the name and authority of Jesus and speak death to the crops of destruction you planted. You can command those seeds to die and command their life source to be cut off so they cannot continue to produce a harvest of destruction to your body.

By the words of your mouth, you are in total control of your harvests, both for evil and for good. In the name of Jesus, speak death and watch the fruits of destruction wither and die; speak life, and you will eat life. After repentance, decree a crop failure where you have sinned against your body and sown the wages of death.

This principle of speaking death and life works on both sides. Speak death where you want to see death. Speak life where you want to see life. Both the power of death and life are in your tongue (Prov. 18:21), and with that power you can change your world. These are the steps of repentance:

1. Confess your sin to God, acknowledging that your sin is against Him (I John 1:9, Psalm 51:2-4).
2. Forgive yourself and refuse to allow your heart to condemn you (I John 3:19-24).
3. If you have wounded someone and it is appropriate, go to him or her, ask forgiveness, and be reconciled (Matthew 5:23-24).
4. Speak death to the fruit of the crops you have sown with your sinful ways (Proverbs 18:21; Galatians 6:7).
5. Speak life where death has been present. Ask the Lord for a specific scripture that will sow life where destruction has been ruling in your life.

Write that scripture here:

_____

_____

My Decree for Today

My body is the temple of the Holy Ghost, and I dedicate it to Him. I say that from this day forward I will quickly repent of every wrong doing, especially acts of wrong doing against my physical body. I choose to conform my life to the Word of God and thank Him for making a way of escape for me. There is great hope for my situation; Jesus has already fixed it!

There is no single thing man can do that brings cleansing and refreshing more than repenting to our ever benevolent Father.

—Brother Lawrence

Day 21

Can I Fix It?

J O U R N A L

My Investment in Wholeness

_____

_____

_____

_____

_____

_____

_____

_____

_____

_____

_____

_____

Day 22

No Disease is Too Hard for Jesus

And Jesus went about all Galilee, teaching in their synagogues, and preaching the gospel of the kingdom, and healing all manner of sickness and all manner of disease among the people (Matthew 4:23).

What are you battling in your body right now? Perhaps you are battling doubt and are having a difficult time believing that God can heal you. Perhaps you have come to believe that your disease is too advanced or your sickness too severe to receive a healing, but I have great news for you. Today's verse says that Jesus heals ALL manner of sickness and disease. ALL. That's pretty conclusive, don't you think? ALL includes whatever is afflicting you.

Have you ever received a healing before, or do you recall a friend or family member who has? Remember, God is the same yesterday, today and forever. His mercy and compassion never fail. Keep your faith high. All you have to lose is your sickness. The Word of God is truth, and there are no exceptions to the truth. God cannot lie, and your situation is not too big for Him. He is ready and willing to lead you into wholeness. Your part is to set your heart and mouth in agreement with what He has already said, and He has much to say about your wholeness. Among other things He has said, "I am the Lord that healeth thee" (Ex. 15:26). Open your mouth and say that so your ears can hear it and your heart can believe it. Say, "God, the Almighty, has healed me." Say, "I am whole and my manifestation is just moments away."

The more you say the words of truth, the quicker your manifestation will come.

The Word cannot fail because it is God Himself. You must set your heart and mouth in agreement with God and what He has already said. Think about it this way: How hard is it to believe in something that has never failed? God has never failed. Getting your healing is as simple as this: just say over and over again, "I know that God can do His job." Say it again, "I know that God can do His job." One more time—"I know that God can do His job." Now let Him.

Ask the Lord for a scripture concerning your own specific healing. Write it here and memorize it.

_____

_____

_____

Write it out on cards and sticky notes and place them where you will see them regularly.

My Decree for Today

Nothing is impossible for God, and I set my faith in Him. He is my Healer, and I know He can and will do His job. I release my faith and give Him full liberty to do whatever He will to bring me into wholeness. I am looking for evidence of a job well done, and I will not be disappointed or denied.

When you say that a situation or person is hopeless, you are slamming the door in the face of God.

—Charles L. Allen

Day 22

No Disease is Too Hard for Jesus

J O U R N A L

My Investment in Wholeness

_____

_____

_____

_____

_____

_____

_____

_____

_____

_____

_____

_____

Day 23

God Watches Over His Word

So shall my word be that goeth forth out of my mouth: it shall not return unto me void, but it shall accomplish that which I please, and it shall prosper in the thing whereto I send it (Is. 55:11).

Then said the Lord unto me, Thou hast well seen: for I will hasten my word to perform it (Jer. 1:12).

Both of our scriptures today take us back to the importance that the Word of God has in our healing. You cannot be healed without it. You must read and hear the Word of God, and you must also speak it. Discipline your mouth to say only what God says about your situation. His Word will not return to Him void, but it will accomplish its mission—not occasionally, but every time.

God promises to hasten to perform His Word, not your word or anyone else's. Again, there is balance in this. Remember the story of the minister in Chapter 3 who added lying to his infirmity? You cannot deny the facts of your illness, but you must openly confess that the Word of God is a higher authority than any symptom in your body. The Word of God must be a part of your daily vocabulary.

During one of my **40 Day** journeys with God, He gave me a special assignment that involved activity that went beyond my normal work schedule. At that time I was battling chronic fatigue, and even though I wanted to do exactly what God expected of me, I didn't believe that I had the strength to do it. I confessed my weakness to the Lord, and He gave me a scripture that literally surged through my body like electricity. That scripture was "...and as thy days, so shall thy strength be" (Deut. 33:25b). That was my promise! I knew God was going to give me all the strength I needed to do what He asked of me.

I took that scripture like medicine every day and faithfully confessed it out of my mouth over and over. I completed that assignment with no stress and without falling behind on any of my other responsibilities. I took the word God had given me and gave it back to Him. He then watched over that word and performed it on my behalf. These are the exact steps you must follow to receive your healing.

- Get the Word of God.
- Give it back to Him by speaking the Word out of your mouth.
- Add faith to the mixture.
- Expect God to manifest His healing power for you.
- Receive your wholeness.

My Decree for Today

God's Word always accomplishes what He sent it to do. He sent His Word to heal me. I agree with that Word and confess from my mouth that my body is whole. The Word knows what to do.

*Read the Bible
to satan and
stay healed.*

—Norvel Hayes

Day 23

God Watches Over His Word

J O U R N A L

My Investment in Wholeness

_____

_____

_____

_____

_____

_____

_____

_____

_____

_____

_____

Day 24

Possess What Belongs to You

Every place that the sole of your foot shall tread upon, that have I given unto you… (Josh. 1:3).

To get the healing your body needs, you are going to have to possess it just as the children of Israel possessed their Promise Land. You're going to have to put your foot on it. It wasn't easy for Joshua and the Israelites to inherit their blessing. They had to go head-to-head with their enemies and make a determined effort to occupy what had been given to them. Three times in Chapter 1 of the Book of Joshua, God told Joshua that in order to possess what rightfully belonged to him, he had to be strong and courageous. The same is true with you. You need to embrace the strength and courage of God and put your foot on your promise of healing.

In most cases sickness and disease do their damage over a long period of time, and sometimes the manifestation of health comes the same way. Your wholeness will work its way out from your inner man and sometimes that process requires patience, strength and courage.

Step out on the Word today, and decree that healing belongs to you and that you will not be denied a full manifestation of everything Jesus died to give you. Often it helps to add actions to your words, so I encourage you to stand up right now and see an imaginary line running across the floor in front of you. The line represents the stripes that Jesus bore for you. Look at the line.

Now I want you to take a big step over that line and as you do, say out loud, "Healing is mine. It belongs to me. I possess it now and I will never again go back to the other side of the stripes." You can do this even if you are unable to stand. Just envision that line and make any effort you can to symbolize walking over it, making your decree as you go. The symbolism is an act to reinforce your faith; it has nothing to do with the effectiveness of your decree.

Now that you've made your decree, never again say anything that is contrary to it. Don't be moved by symptoms, or time, or what others say or anything else. Stand firm where you have put your foot because it's on His promise according to our verse today, "Every place the sole of your foot shall tread, that I have (past tense) given unto you."

This is a good time to begin planning your victory celebration. In today's journal I encourage you to write down something special you want to do when your healing manifests. Get a vision of that celebration in your heart, and be as specific as possible. Great celebrations take planning, so get started. Your day of celebration is almost here.

My Decree for Today

I've walked across the bloody stripes
That paid the price for me.
Healing is my portion
And my body is set free.
Never again will I say
That I am weak or sick or sore
Because I am completely healed
By the stripes that Jesus bore.

It is vain to wait for God to do what He has commanded you to do, and He has commanded mankind to freely take all He has given.

—A. W. Tozer

Day 24

Possess What Belongs to You

J O U R N A L

My Investment in Wholeness

_____

_____

_____

_____

_____

_____

_____

_____

_____

_____

Day 25

Ask What Ye Will

If ye abide in me, and my words abide in you, ye shall ask what ye will, and it shall be done unto you (John 15:7).

Medical science aids healing through natural means such as medication, therapies, treatments or surgeries. All of these things use natural principles, fashioned in the natural realm, to produce a natural result. God's divine healing is not natural; it's spiritual and is ministered through your spirit man. Divine healing comes from the inside out.

Just as you would take natural medicine to aid your healing by a natural means, so you must take the Word of God concerning healing to aid your healing by a spiritual means. Today's verse says that you must abide in Jesus and allow His Words to abide in you. *To abide* means to dwell and to rest in that dwelling. God's Word can't abide in you and bring you rest if you don't put it into your heart. I cannot emphasize enough the importance of reading your Bible. You must be convinced by the Word of God that it is His will to heal you. You will never be able to ask for divine healing and claim it by faith if you don't know for certain exactly what God offers.

I can boldly say that the most common reason people fail to receive their healing is the lack of God's Word in their heart. If you do not spend committed time "abiding" in the Word, you do not meet the criteria set out in today's scripture for asking Jesus to heal you. I have come to realize in every area of my own life where I suffer lack, that lack is primarily due to a deficit of God's Word in my heart. To know without a doubt what God has said about your healing is the only sufficient evidence you have to appropriate true faith. To receive from God you must know His Word and plant it as seed in your life. Until you can say, "It is Written," and then quote to the adversary what God has said about your situation, your faith cannot remain steadfast, and you will not see a harvest.

Before saying, "I AM the Lord that healeth thee," and promising to take away all your sicknesses, God first said, "If thou wilt hearken… and do all." This means to be diligent in the matter of knowing His Word and practicing what it says.

List three "It is written" statements from the Word of God that apply to your healing and declare them to the enemy:

1. It is written _____

_____

2. It is written _____

_____

3. It is written _____

_____

My Decree for Today

I say that I am a pursuer of truth, and in that pursuit I commit to read and study God's Word daily. I will pursue the Word until I possess my place of rest, and I will dwell there all the days of my life.

*Feed your faith
and your doubts will
starve to death.*

—Abraham Lincoln

Day 25

Ask What Ye Will

JOURNAL

My Investment in Wholeness

Day 26

Stop Signing For the Package

Seeing then that we have a great high priest that is passed into the heavens, Jesus the Son of God; let us hold fast our profession. For we have not an high priest which cannot be touched with the feeling of our infirmities... (Heb. 4:14-15).

Jesus is our high priest, and He has made health and wholeness readily available to all who will believe. The word profession in today's scripture is better translated as confession. It means to acknowledge and openly express something. It is a fixed spiritual principle that what you speak from your lips controls your life. You will never rise above your confession. So what should you confess? What should you acknowledge and openly express?

You should express and hold fast to the undeniable integrity of God's Word. You should confess things like, "God is my strength and shield. He is my very present help in the time of trouble." You should confess that you are standing firm on all that Jesus has done for you, especially in the face of all contrary evidence. Eph. 4:29 tells you to only speak that which is good and edifying. In the original Greek, this verse is written in the command tense meaning that this is not a suggestion; it is a command. You are commanded to permit only edifying words to come out of your mouth. When the enemy tempts you to say something other than what God has said, don't sign for the package. Boldly mark across it: *Return to Sender.*

When you speak a negative confession about your circumstances, you lower yourself to the level of that confession. Your words will imprison you if they are negative and will set you free if they are positive. Your wrong confession shuts Jesus out and lets satan in. When you confess your sickness, you are actually confessing that you believe more in that sickness than you believe in God. Don't get caught up in that. Every word you speak is vital to your well-being, and you must diligently guard every word that comes out of your mouth. Every time you confess something contrary to the Word of God, you deny His ability and willingness to help you.

"Thou art snared with the words of thy mouth, thou art taken with the words of thy mouth." (Prov. 6:2)

Sickness and disease gain ascendancy when you confess the testimony of your senses. Your body becomes trapped by your very words. Feelings and appearances have no place in the realm of faith. Confessing your sickness is like signing for a package from FedEx. Your words are the signed receipt satan has to prove that you accepted what he sent you. Give no place to the devil.

Check the box if you have "signed for any of these packages."

❑ Fear   _____
❑ Disease and infirmity   _____
❑ A medical diagnosis   _____
❑ Death   _____

Now go back and boldly mark each one *Return to Sender*

My Decree for Today

My mouth is filled with truth and the goodness of the Lord. I say that life and wholeness are mine and I walk in nothing less. I cast down every vain thought and reasoning that would come against the Word of God concerning my healing, and I say that I am whole and my manifestation is imminent.

Confession always goes ahead of healing. Don't watch the symptoms, watch the Word.

—E.W. Kenyon

Day 26

Stop Signing For the Package

J O U R N A L

My Investment in Wholeness

_____

_____

_____

_____

_____

_____

_____

_____

_____

_____

_____

_____

_____

_____

Day 27

Guard Your Heart

Keep thy heart with all diligence; for out of it are the issues of life (Prov. 4: 23).

The issues of your life are the things you give out of your life and our verse today says that all of those things come from your heart. The word heart in this passage refers to your soul, which is the seat of your intellect, reasoning, free will and emotions. Each of these things must be guarded with diligence… with persistent, painstaking effort.

Every decision you make originates in the inner depth of the heart of your soul. After a decision is made, an action will follow. Let's continue reading in Proverbs Chapter 4 as Solomon tells you what keeping and guarding your heart involves:

Put away from thee a forward mouth and perverse lips put far from thee. Let thine eyes look right on, and let thine eyelids look straight before thee. Ponder the paths of thy feet, and let all thy ways be established (Prov. 4: 24-26).

Two things are very important in these verses: first, that keeping your heart is your responsibility, and secondly, that the Holy Spirit tells you the three specific things you must watch:

- What you say
- What you see
- Where you go

It is imperative to have a pure heart before the Lord if you are to receive a release of wholeness to your body. Wholeness and holiness are synonymous. To be whole you must take full responsibility to guard the words that come out of your mouth, guard what you allow your eyes to see and guard where you allow your feet to go.

Guarding your heart with all diligence causes the outflow of your life to be pure and puts you in position to receive healing and everything else God has for you. Set your heart on God, ask Him to help you guard it, and move into wholeness.

Think about what you have been saying.

What have you been putting before your eyes?

Where have you been going?

If your life is not disciplined in these areas, then repent. Ask the Holy Spirit to put a guard on your heart today. Then obey the Lord because He will surely reveal to you any areas of your speech, senses and walk that do not please Him.

For another look at guarding your heart, I recommend that you see the back of this book for ordering information on additional materials on this subject. See *Where Is Your Heart?*

My Decree for Today

I put my hope and faith in God and trust Him with all I am and all I will ever be. I choose to put a guard over my heart so that I can fulfill my life's purpose and be fruitful in the Kingdom of God.

*Every decision and
action flow out of the
inner attitudes and
choices of our heart.
Putting a guard over
that well is our own
responsibility.*

—Freeda Bowers

Day 27

Guard Your Heart

journal My Investment in Wholeness

_____

_____

_____

_____

_____

_____

_____

_____

_____

_____

_____

_____

Day 28

Send the Invitation

Call unto Me, and I will answer thee, and show thee great and mighty things, which thou knowest not (Jer. 33:3).

oday's verse brings to light a very simple part of the healing process that we sometimes overlook. The Lord spoke to Jeremiah and said, "Call unto Me." That word "call" has the connotation of extending an invitation. Have you invited the Lord to lead you into healing, or have you begged and pleaded with Him to just do something? There is a big difference between the two. Only calling upon the Lord will open the doors of revelation to the great and mighty things that you know nothing about but surely need. Begging is a sign of unbelief, and when God hears it He turns a deafened ear.

Our Lord is a King and should always be treated in a kingly fashion. Americans especially have difficulty relating to royalty. In a nation ruled by royalty, the subjects would never demand anything of the king. It would only be with great humility that they would make their petitions known before him. They would never be arrogant or complaining. They would never appear before the king disheveled or out of turn. They would wait for his bidding before they entered His presence and be honored that he granted them an audience.

How have you approached the Lord with your needs? Have you spent much of your prayer time telling Him about every ache and pain you have and about how inadequate your doctors are? Have you whined and cried and complained? God is not moved by your need; He's moved by your faith. So, I encourage you to revisit how you have talked to Him about your situation.

Today, make a fresh commitment and start on a new path. Begin to invite the King to oversee your work as you master the tools of the great treasure of His Word. Let your heart prepare a way for Him to come and do the work He longs to do. Prepare for the King as you would for royalty. He desires to work with you to bring about a full release of all you need today. Invite the King of kings to come. Call upon Him, and He will show you things you have never thought possible.

Below, list three ways that you can change how you prepare your heart before the Lord to approach Him as the royalty that He is. Implement those changes today.

_____

_____

_____

_____

My Decree for Today

I am preparing a grand and elegant invitation for the King of the universe. I am inviting Him to join me in the place of faith. We will meet there together, and as He sits enthroned upon my heart, health and wholeness will be released to my body. The King of kings knows my invitation is coming, and He anxiously awaits its arrival. I am sending it out today.

You are a person of great faith. You either have faith in your sickness, or faith in God's power to heal you. I hope for your sake your faith is in the right thing.

—Kenneth E. Hagin

Day 28

Send the Invitation

J O U R N A L

My Investment in Wholeness

_____

_____

_____

_____

_____

_____

_____

_____

_____

_____

_____

Day 29

Did God Make Me Sick?

Also every sickness and every plague, which is not written in this book of the law, them will I bring upon thee, until thou be destroyed (Deut. 28:61).

Many people believe that God gave them their sickness and scriptures like the one we have for today seem to support that belief. Today, I want us to explore what God REALLY said to the Israelites in this passage.

The Old Testament was originally written in the Hebrew language, which has idioms that cannot be translated into English. In transcribing the original manuscripts into English, the King James translators chose the nearest possible words for translation as they wrote the Bible we use today, but in a few cases their best choice was far from accurate. Today's verse falls into that category.

A brilliant and anointed Bible scholar by the name of Dr. Robert Young helps clarify this verse. In his book, *Young's Analytical Concordance to the Bible*, Dr. Young explains that the King James translators did not understand the causative and permissive verbs that were commonly used in the original writings of the Bible. Dr. Young says that this verse in Deuteronomy should have been translated with a permissive verb, thus making it read, "Every sickness and plague, which is not written in the book of the law, them will the Lord allow to ascend upon thee until thou be destroyed." Big difference!

God is not the source of your sickness, but He does grant permission to the devil to put sickness on you—not from the standpoint of punishment, but from the standpoint of your delegated authority. God allows sickness because you do. You have the power to agree with sickness or to deny it the right to be on your body. What will your choice be? Trust me; you don't have to think about this twice, but in case you're still confused, let me help you... Choose life.

I encourage you to meditate particularly on today's quotes. These men of God know the strength of His Word.

My Decree for Today

I take the authority Jesus has given me and I refuse to allow sickness and disease to afflict me any longer. I am whole in Christ, and I stand in agreement with that wholeness. Nothing outside of a body filled with the life of Jesus is acceptable to me.

So you think God made you sick? Let me ask you a question. Where did He get it? There is no sickness in heaven.

—Kenneth Copeland

If you think God made you sick, it is a sin to see a doctor to make you well.

—T. L. Osborn

Day 29

Did God Make Me Sick?

J O U R N A L

My Investment in Wholeness

_____

_____

_____

_____

_____

_____

_____

_____

_____

_____

_____

_____

Day 30

Divine Healing vs. Divine Health

And they overcame him by the blood of the Lamb, and by the word of their testimony (Rev. 12:11).

It is wonderful to get healed when you are sick, but there is something available for you far greater than healing. It is divine health.

John G. Lake, an anointed healing evangelist once said, "Divine healing is the removal by the power of God of the disease that has come upon the body. Divine health is to live day by day, hour by hour, in touch with God so that the Life of God flows into the body just as the Life of God flows into the mind or flows into the spirit."

Your walk with God is a progressive journey. As a believer in Jesus, you are already entitled to all things He has provided, but you only receive them as you are perfected in His love for you. God sees you in right standing with Jesus, but manifesting the fullness of that in your life requires trust and a willing obedience on your part, and the steps of that journey are always the same:

You hear the Word of God.
You speak the Word of God.
You believe the Word of God.
You speak the Word of God.
You receive the Word of God.
You testify of the goodness of God.

Once you obtain a provision of the covenant, you start the process all over again. You must make the steps and make them in order. Charles Capps puts it this way: "You can't put a third story on a vacant lot." You can't get a healing without first building a foundation for it from the Word of God. If you build a building, you have to start at the ground level. If you want a harvest, you have to plant something first. The only place that success comes before work is in the dictionary.

You should be continually growing in the truths of the kingdom, taking everything you receive at one level with you as you journey to the next. In God, nothing you gain is lost. It just develops into something higher and more glorious.

As you seek a healing for your body, I encourage you to not let that be your ultimate goal for there is something far greater than healing. It is God's plan and purpose that you live in divine health. Just as the millions of Israelites left Egypt with no sickness or disease among them (Ps. 105:37), it is God's plan that His Church be the same as she exits this life. Whether you enter heaven by way of death or by way of the rapture, it is God's plan that you go healthy. Embrace your covenant of health and push beyond the healing you need for today to obtain the greater thing—divine health. What is the difference between divine health and healing?

_____

_____

My Decree for Today

I see myself completely whole, filled with the life of Christ and living in divine health. I commit to continually search the Word of God for all He has for me and receive it as a living reality.

You can have good, better or best. You can have healing, health or wholeness. That's a pretty simple choice, don't you think?

—F.F. Bosworth, Author of *Christ the Healer*

Day 30

Divine Healing vs. Divine Health

My Investment in Wholeness

_____

_____

_____

_____

_____

_____

_____

_____

_____

_____

Testimony

A friend introduced me to your book, **Give Me 40 Days**, and I decided to give God **40 Days**, believing Him to control my diabetes and weight problem. My sugar levels were running as high as 400-450. Shortly after I completed the **40 Days,** I began waking up with normal sugar levels. I am now consistently waking up with sugar levels between 89-119. Thanks to God! I have also been slowly losing weight. I know I will reach my weight goal and continue to keep my sugar levels under control.

—JM, Texas

Day 31

Confess Your Faults

Confess your faults one to another, and pray one for another, that ye may be healed. The effectual fervent prayer of a righteous man availeth much (James 5:16).

e have often heard the last portion of this scripture quoted, but how many times have you heard about confessing your faults to one another? Probably not too many—I know that I haven't. We tend to be selective when quoting the Word of God. We only say the positive parts. I doubt if you have, "Confess your faults one to another…" posted on your refrigerator or have discussed it with your family members lately, but confession is healthy and can be an important part of receiving divine healing.

I do not interpret this verse the way some religions do, expecting you to report all of your wrong doings to another person who will absolve you of your sin. No one has the power to forgive sin but Jesus Christ, and He is the only one you need to go to for atonement of your sin. I do believe, however, that we need to make ourselves accountable to other believers who will instruct us and pray for us when we battle sin and the weaknesses of our flesh. It is important that we be transparent with our brothers and sisters in Christ.

How does this work when pursuing a healing for your body? First you need to recognize that this is about you. Notice that today's verse says, "Confess your faults." It doesn't say, "Confess your neighbors' faults." You must guard your mouth and refuse to speak evil about anyone. Your mother always said, "If you can't say something nice, say nothing at all," and her words are particularly applicable now.

Your healing is going to come through the words of your mouth, and your failure to receive healing will come the same way. So, avoid the temptation to discuss the shortcomings of others. That's between them and God.

As for your own shortcomings, be quick to confess your weaknesses to someone you trust, especially in areas that affect your faith. If, for example, a manifestation of healing isn't coming quickly, and you are battling doubt and unbelief, confess that to another believer. Just saying out of your mouth, "I'm having a hard time believing for my healing," will set in motion a force of the Spirit to strengthen you and get you back on track.

Make a list of three weaknesses or shortcomings that you would like to be able to confess to a trusted, believing friend in order to get prayer support and accountability in these areas, so that healing can come.

_____

_____

_____

My Decree for Today

I make the choice to no longer hide my weaknesses from those who love me in Christ. As the Holy Spirit prompts me, I will endeavor to be transparent and accountable to others and confess my faults.

*Keeping secrets is a
bondage that can take
you to an early grave
because what is kept in
secret rots.*

—Watchman Nee

Day 31

Confess Your Faults

J O U R N A L

My Investment in Wholeness

Day 32

You Are Not Judge or Jury

For if ye forgive men their trespasses, your heavenly Father will also forgive you: But if ye forgive not men their trespasses, neither will your Father forgive your trespasses (Matt. 6:14-15).

Forbearing one another, and forgiving one another, if any man have a quarrel against any: even as Christ forgave you, so also do ye (Col. 3:13).

The enemy will be masterful in his attempts to keep you from receiving healing. He has a truckload full of obstacles to throw your way as you progress along these **40 Days**. You must determine that you will not be deterred by anything he sends. There is one matter, however, you need to look at closely that is not an obstacle from the enemy, but one you create for yourself. Our scripture today addresses this issue.

Holding unforgiveness in your heart builds a barrier that will prevent a release of healing. You must be willing to forgive everyone who has ever wounded, used, betrayed or violated you and release him or her to the Lord. Vengeance belongs only to God, and you have no legal right in Jesus to do anything but love those in your life. You cannot obey the love commandment and hold unforgiveness against them.

Sin is often the open door for sickness and disease. Sin may be the open door in your life, and if so, you surely need God's forgiveness of that sin before anything else will happen to release healing to you. Today's verse says that if you fail to forgive others, God will not forgive you. That means if you are holding unforgiveness in your heart toward another person, there is no way to close the open door to your illness. If you can't release the one who sinned against you, God cannot forgive you of the very sin that opened your life to sickness.

Forgiveness is not a feeling. It is an act of obedience. In Matt. 6:14, Jesus says that the Father will only forgive you of sin if you forgive others. That's a sobering thought. If you will not forgive those who have wounded you, your prayers of repentance fall on deaf ears in heaven. Without a doubt, you must be able to appropriate the cleansing, atoning Blood of Jesus everyday, but especially if you need a manifestation of healing in your body. The forgiveness that brings release of healing to your physical body is not available to you if you have unforgiveness in your heart.

Forgiveness is not an option. Forgiving those who hurt you is a requirement of every believer in Jesus Christ. Since forgiveness is a decision and not a feeling, you must simply decide to obey the Word of God.

And be ye kind one to another, tenderhearted, forgiving one another, even as God for Christ's sake has forgiven you (Eph. 4:32).

Think about this for a moment. Where would you be today if God chose to hold all of your offenses against you? What would your outcome be if He refused to forgive you? You would be in unbelievable bondage and suffer unbearable and continual loss. God's forgiveness is what gives you the ability to thrive and know peace in this life. What could possibly be worth losing that? If you refuse to forgive someone who has hurt you, you gain nothing and you compound your loss. You not only have the pain of the original injury, you have a barrier between you and God who truly loves you and can heal you.

When you have been wounded by another person, your emotions can be raw and your mind will give you countless reasons why you have the right to hold a grudge. You will find it easy to justify your feelings and most of the people you know will agree that you have every right to be angry and perhaps even vindictive. That's the natural side of things, but God's perspective is entirely different. You must forgive.

Who has hurt you the most in your lifetime? Who has caused you the most pain? Write their names on the lines below. You can write the names of people both living and dead. If you need more lines, use the journal pages for today.

_____   _____

_____   _____

_____   _____

_____   _____

_____   _____

_____   _____

Do you want to be completely whole? Do you want it badly enough to forgive the people whose names you've written on the lines above? You can't have it both ways. You have to make a choice. You can either harbor unforgiveness in your heart and mind and remain sick, or you can forgive those who have hurt you and begin to heal. Because you become accountable in God for what you know, realize that from this day forward, you will experience even greater than before the consequences of disobedience if you choose not to forgive. So, what will your choice be? I only see that you have one choice. You must forgive.

Go back to each name and, one at a time, do the following: look at the name and say it out loud. Say the name again. Even if you don't "feel" like it, do it totally as an act of obedience, look at the name as you say the following out loud:

"(Name the person) _____, I forgive you for all you have done to me. As an act of my will I choose to release you to Jesus. Whatever He wills for you is sufficient for me. I will never again hold unforgiveness in my heart toward you. Be free."

Please say that one more time. Now get a pen with a different-colored ink than you have been using, preferably red. Look at the name again and say the following:

"(Name the person) _____, I forgive you completely and put you under the Blood of Jesus Christ, and I ask Him to heal you of all of the hurts in you that caused you to hurt me."

Now take your second pen and mark through the name as a symbol that he or she is under the Blood of Jesus and that what was done to you is under the Blood, too, never to surface again.

One last thing—pray this: "Father, in Jesus' name I ask that You forgive me for sitting as judge and jury over _____ . I will never do it again. Amen

You may feel a tremendous relief right away, and you may feel nothing for quite awhile. Your feelings are irrelevant. Remember that forgiveness is an act of obedience. One day soon you will have a complete assurance from God that this has been a life-defining moment for you.

My Decree for Today

I am free. I am free. Nothing can hold me. I refuse to harbor unforgiveness against anyone and nothing can steal my quality of life or my wholeness in Jesus. I am forgiven by His mercy and covered in His Blood. I am free.

There are two distinct marks of a genuine Christian, giving and forgiving. If both are not apparent, the validity of one's relationship with Jesus should be seriously questioned.

—Freeda Bowers

Day 32

You Are Not Judge or Jury

J O U R N A L

My Investment in Wholeness

_____

_____

_____

_____

_____

_____

_____

_____

_____

_____

_____

Day 33

Healing is In Your Mouth

The Word is nigh thee, even in thy mouth, and in thy heart: That is, the word of faith which we preach (Rom. 10:8).

Your physical body has no nature of its own. It is just flesh, blood and bone and it only does what it is trained to do. Your body receives the majority of its training from the words of your own mouth. Your words give instructions to your body, and eventually your immune system responds to your words. Either health or sickness is the result. You don't need to talk God into healing your body; you need to talk your body into receiving the healing that has already been bought for you.

To have victory over your body you have to make a decision from which there is no retreat. You must make a heart commitment to never argue with the Word of God concerning your health, and then keep your word. This is a decision God will not make for you. He set before you life and death and told you to choose life. He has done all He's going to do. You must respond to His invitation and immediately put a guard over your mouth and carefully watch everything you say.

How many times have you said things like these?

"My feet are killing me."   "I'm taking a cold."   "This virus will be the death of me."

You must never say things like that again. God's way is to call for life and wholeness in your body, even if they are not yet a natural reality. There is probably no other subject as important to healing as the principle of calling things that are not as though they are (Rom. 4:17). This one principle could be the key to an immediate manifestation of healing in your body.

You must ignore your symptoms and speak over your body what God says about it and continue to do that until your healing manifests. Exercise the power that resides in your mouth. There are no drugs or therapies more powerful against whatever has attacked your body than the Word of God spoken in faith out of your own mouth.

You have heard much in the news about weapons of mass destruction. I assure you there are no greater weapons of destruction than faith-filled words coming from the mouth of a child of God. The words of health to your body and the words of death to the assignments of the enemy against your body are both in your mouth. Speak up.

My Decree for Today

I am well armed against all sickness and disease, and I will not hesitate to use my weapons of mass destruction against everything that comes to rob me of my covenant rights. My mouth is filled with good things, and I will speak them over my body, expecting an immediate manifestation of healing.

*It is much wiser
to choose what you
say than to say what
you choose.*

—Unknown

Day 33

Healing is In Your Mouth

J O U R N A L

My Investment in Wholeness

_____

_____

_____

_____

_____

_____

_____

_____

_____

_____

_____

Day 34

Be Led of the Spirit

Are ye so foolish? Having begun in the Spirit, are ye now made perfect by the flesh? (Gal. 3:3).

Every provision of the covenant belongs to you, but none of them will come to you automatically. You live in a physical body that was created in a fallen nature. Your spirit-man is created in the image of God, but your soul-man and your physical body are created in the image of fallen man, Adam (Genesis 5:3). The key to covenant living is found in learning how to allow your spirit-man to respond to the Holy Spirit. Everything begins and is perfected in the Spirit, and you must be Spirit-led, not controlled by your fallen nature. Being Spirit-led means allowing the Holy Spirit to dictate your actions and reactions in life.

As you walk in the Spirit, the demands of your natural man will have less and less power over you. It doesn't work the other way around. You don't get your flesh under control and then walk in the Spirit. You make a decision to get the Word of God into your heart and constantly speak that Word out of your mouth. I don't mean that you should start talking in King James English, but cause your speech to agree with what God has said. As you make the Word of God the final authority in your life, your natural man, meaning your intellect, reasoning and physical body will begin to align themselves to righteousness.

God is asking you now to believe His Word and receive health in your body so that you can become an instrument to demonstrate His reality to the lost. Allow the Holy Spirit to guide you into all truth. Make your daily decisions based upon

His promptings, not upon what your natural eyes see or your natural ears hear. God wants to give you greater spiritual authority so that you might be about His business and glorify His name.

You already possess great authority in Jesus Christ, but you must be led of the Spirit to use it. The Holy Spirit is ready to equip you, teach you and impart to you all that you need. Yield to His leading in your life. Surrender your rights to be in control. If you do not surrender those rights, the Holy Spirit will never usurp them. God wants to release a whole army of believers to live in the dimension of divine health and to compel others to follow behind them. Could that be you? It IS you, if you choose to join up.

I encourage you to embrace the vision that God has a plan for your life and wants to use you. Allow the Holy Spirit to propel you through the process of receiving your healing and on into divine health and to plant you in the place of the miraculous. God wants you to step over into your calling and demonstrate the fullness of His goodness to the world.

Your part is to be willing and obedient. Invite the Holy Spirit to come and baptize you with the power to live a life led by the Spirit.

My Decree for Today

I say that I will not die, but live, and declare the works of the Lord (Ps. 118:17). I will be yielded to the Holy Spirit and not try to work out the answers to my needs in my own strength. I am on an assignment from the King Eternal and Holy, and I will fulfill all He requires of me. What is begun in the Spirit will end that way because I surrender to God's plan for my life.

God can be no bigger in your life than you confess Him to be. Confess that He is your Shepherd and that you want not.

—Freeda Bowers

Day 34

Be Led of the Spirit

J O U R N A L

My Investment in Wholeness

_____

_____

_____

_____

_____

_____

_____

_____

_____

_____

_____

Day 35

Hire the Guards

Finally, brethren, whatsoever things are true, whatsoever things are honest, whatsoever things are just, whatsoever things are pure, whatsoever things are lovely, whatsoever things are of good report: If there be any virtue, and if there be any praise, think on these things (Phil. 4:8).

By now it should be very clear to you that the words of your mouth play a vital part in your healing process. You can speak either life or death over your situation and whatever you say is exactly what you will get.

In today's scripture, the Apostle Paul reveals the things that should rule our hearts and lives. He mentions six things specifically that should be apparent in the life of every believer. I see this scripture in picture form. I see six strong security guards standing at the door of my mouth. I see that each guard addresses each word that comes out of my mouth and asks it a question. If the word can answer the question positively, it can pass to the next guard. If the word can pass all six of the guards, then and only then, can it leave my mouth.

What questions do these guards ask? They demand that each word that passes through my mouth positively respond to the following:

Is it true?
Is it honest?
It is just?
Is it pure?
Is it lovely?
Is it a good report?

If you would simply attempt to submit the words of your mouth to the scrutiny of these gatekeepers, your soul would prosper and your body would respond with health and wholeness. Every facet of your life would be purer and more prosperous. It may seem like an incredibly high standard to live up to the demands of these gatekeepers, but oh, how sweet will be the reward if you will give them permission to stand guard over your words.

Again, your healing is going to come through the words of your mouth, and if you fail to receive healing, your loss will come the same way. This takes us back to what I mentioned earlier about the admonition of your mother when she said, "If you can't say something nice, say nothing at all." Listen to your mother. Listen to me, and put those big bodyguards on payroll today.

Have you hired the guards? Repent for past words of gossip and slander and words that bring destruction to you and others, and write about ways that you can change what you say. Instead of saying: _____

_____ as I have been, I will now say _____ or else nothing at all. Repeat this in your journal as many times as needed to get your words in line with those guards you have placed on your heart and mouth.

My Decree for Today

My words are powerful weapons against sickness and are the keys to releasing the wellspring of the life that dwells within me. I choose to allow the Word of God to dictate what I say, and I commit to be silent if I cannot decree the goodness of my God.

Medical doctors measure physical health by how the tongue looks. The Great Physician measures spiritual health by how the tongue acts.

—Unknown

Day 35

Hire the Guards

J O U R N A L

My Investment in Wholeness

_____

_____

_____

_____

_____

_____

_____

_____

_____

_____

_____

_____

Day 36

Your Future is Stored in Your Heart

A good man out of the good treasure of his heart bringeth forth good things; and an evil man out of the evil treasure bringeth forth evil things (Matt. 12:35).

God has already done all He is going to do to bring healing to your body. Jesus is not going to take one more stripe so that your disease will go away. He has already borne all the stripes He will ever bear, and your sickness and disease are already gone.

Your connection with God and what He has already done for you will come from your heart. Your future is stored there. Until your heart is filled with truth and you set your mouth in agreement with that truth, the wonderful gift of divine health that has already been given to you will remain an arm's length away. For faith to work it has to be in two places… in your heart and in your mouth. If you fill your heart with the good treasure of the truth concerning your healing, and speak that truth out of your mouth, you will see a manifestation in your physical body.

There can be obstacles that will keep you from walking in faith. Bitterness and offense are two major things that will put up barriers that can cause you to fail to receive a release of your healing. Refuse to allow your heart to become bitter or hardened because people or circumstances are not lining up to your expectations. You may be disappointed or angry with some of the people in your life. You may have placed false expectations upon those around you by expecting things from them that only Jesus can give you. When we expect people to meet our needs, we limit Jesus in what He can do on our behalf, and the people become burdened and discouraged. Ask God to reveal if you are guilty of placing a burden on others by yoking them with false expectations. If so, repent, ask their forgiveness and move on. It will be freeing for you, and freeing for them. Keep your heart clean.

One of the best rules of thumb in our relationships with all people is found in Phil.2:2b: "…Let each esteem others better than themselves."

This verse is not written as a request but as a command, and although I try to make it a standard in my life, I can assure you it's easier said than done. Your physical condition may be such that you are dependent upon others to assist with your care. I encourage you to remember this verse and apply it to those around you. Don't be demanding or short-tempered. Esteem those helping you by expressing your gratitude for all they do for you and by giving back to them in whatever way you can.

If you want your external condition to change, you must change your internal condition. You do that by expressing the love of Jesus, by putting His Word in your heart and speaking it out of your mouth. You need to deposit God's Word into your heart just like you would deposit money in a bank. If you have nothing deposited in your heart, there will be nothing to withdraw. Hardening of the heart ages people more quickly than hardening of the arteries. Only the Gospel of Jesus Christ can break hardened hearts and heal broken ones, so store up for your future and give yourself a regular diet of the Gospel.

Don't put them off. This is the day for depositing these things. This is the day that the Lord has made. Don't face another day bankrupt of God's tangible presence in your life.

My Decree for Today

I am robed in righteousness, and out of the abundance of my heart I will speak only truth and life. I will be faithful to deposit the treasure of the Word of God into my heart, and out of my mouth I will speak that Word and will see a full manifestation of wholeness in my life.

Walking in love releases all the benefits of love into your life. That's a pretty good deal because God is love and when you act like Him you get all He is.

—Gloria Copeland

Day 36

Your Future is Stored in Your Heart

J O U R N A L

My Investment in Wholeness

_____

_____

_____

_____

_____

_____

_____

_____

_____

_____

Day 37

The Laying on of Hands

Now when the sun was setting, all they that had any sick with divers diseases brought them unto him; and he laid his hands on every one of them, and healed them (Luke 4:40).

We see throughout the Gospels that Jesus predominantly healed by using one of two means... sometimes both. He either spoke to, or laid His hands upon the person afflicted. The ministry of the laying on of hands is valid and still in operation today. Jesus has given to those who will commit their lives to Him and follow in His ways the authority to do the same works He did.

I encourage you to find someone who believes in divine healing and ask him or her to agree with you for a manifestation of healing in your body. As the two of you come together in agreement, ask that person to lay his or her hands on you. Do not put your faith in the person but keep it centered in Jesus. Always keep in the forefront of your mind that Jesus is the Healer. The person praying is only an instrument who can assist you in receiving a release of your healing.

It is somewhat like a midwife assisting a pregnant mother in labor. The mother still has to do the work, but the midwife is there to assist her and make the process easier. It is your own faith that will make you whole. Another person can add their faith to yours in a number of ways, one of which is the laying on of hands. Remember, there is a difference between healing and wholeness and you can receive a healing though the faith of another without adding any faith of your own. Many who have not been taught the ways of faith are healed that way, but you can only be made whole, or in other words obtain divine health, by your own faith.

When I was carrying our son, Victor, I came down with a serious kidney infection. I had been running high fevers and was very ill. One day at church, I was in great pain and mentioned it to my pastor's wife before service. During praise and worship, she came to me and prayed for me. At that moment I felt nothing, but by the end of the service my faith had risen to such a place that when I walked out the door I knew I was healed. As Claud and I walked up to our home, I told him that I knew I was healed. Indeed I was. The infection left immediately and never returned.

You will need the wisdom of God in finding the right person to ask to lay hands on you. I would not do this without first knowing the spiritual integrity of the person you ask, and I wouldn't do it until I knew that his or her faith is at the level of yours or greater. The purpose of laying on of hands is to impart to you a measure of faith that can cause a multiplication in what you already have. In God, one plus one does not make two. God does not do addition. In Him all things multiply, and His multiplication tables don't resemble ours at all.

"One can chase a thousand, and two *(the power of agreement)* can put ten thousand to flight" (Deut. 32:30). *The added emphasis is mine.*

In God, one plus one (meaning two people set in agreement) equals 10,000. I like those odds, don't you? It's somewhat like a fixed race.

According to Luke 4: 40, how did healing flow through Jesus?

_____

According to Mark 16:18b, how will healing flow through a believer?

_____

My Decree for Today

I am filled with faith for my healing and will gratefully receive an impartation from the one God sends to lay hands on me.

Have confidence in His servant or prophet, but put your faith in Almighty God, not man.

—Oral Roberts

Day 37

The Laying on of Hands

J O U R N A L

My Investment in Wholeness

_____

_____

_____

_____

_____

_____

_____

_____

_____

_____

_____

_____

_____

Day 38

What Will You Wear?

Let nothing be done through strife or vainglory; but in lowliness of mind let each esteem other better than themselves (Phil. 2: 3).

We have talked about the importance of praying for others as you take this **40 Day** journey with God. It is necessary that you get your mind off of yourself, and praying for others is a great way to do that. I would like for you to dedicate this day to praying for someone beside yourself. You cannot be selfish and pray for someone else. The selfless acts you do are important for a number of reasons, and I would like to look at one of them today. Removing yourself from selfishness is an act of humility. It is only the humble that God exalts, not those who are consumed with themselves.

I have a friend who had a spiritual dream several years ago. In the dream, God gave her a powerful and poignant message. My friend dreamed that she was giving her whole heart to serve someone who was ungrateful, hateful and cruel. The other person was a bride preparing for her wedding, and my friend was trying to help her get dressed in a magnificent gown. Nothing my friend did to help this bride pleased her. She was vulgar and arrogant. Several other things happened in the dream, but what I want to share with you here is how the dream ended. At the end, my friend was wearing the wedding gown and it was more spectacular than anything she had ever seen. She was the one who was getting married.

The Lord gave this interpretation to the dream. He said that many would desire to wear the wedding gown that will clothe His Bride, but only a specific group would be fit to wear it. He said only those who are true servants will be dressed in this gown on the day of the Marriage of the Lamb, for the only bridal garment that will be acceptable on that day is the garment of humility.

Serving others, or as our verse for today says, "esteeming others higher than yourself…" is an act of humility. The scriptures tell us that the Bride of Christ will dress herself. What will you wear on the day of the great wedding? When you pray for someone else, you are acting as a servant to that person, and you are working on the preparation of your bridal garment.

Standing in the gap for the needs of another person releases so many wonderful things to you, and healing is one of them. "Pray ye one for another that ye may be healed" (James 5:16).

As you pray for someone else today, God doesn't want you to take on his or her care. He is the burden bearer. When you take on the weight of someone else's problem, you are trying to take the place of Jesus in his or her life. You are not created to carry that kind of load and can actually get in God's way. Your place is to confess the life and wholeness of Jesus over that person, just as you are learning to do for yourself, not become consumed with their problem.

Being a servant in God's household isn't laborious or painful. His yoke is easy, and His burden is light. If you feel that you are becoming heavy-hearted or worried about the one you pray for, you have stepped over into a place you don't belong. Just stop. Praise the Lord for that person and ask Him to correct your steps. He will.

What God taught me in my first **40 Days** remains true today. There is such a refreshing in praying for others that I rarely pray for my own needs. I mostly pray for others and thank God for taking care of me. I encourage you to do the same. It is a glorious and worry-free way to live!

My Decree for Today

My heart is as Your heart, Lord. My heart is for others. I trust You to care for Me as You entrust me to intercede for those unable to pray for themselves. Thank You for this great privilege, and thank You for releasing the healing that is in me.

Humility is like underwear. We should all have it...but not let it show.

—Unknown

Day 38

What Will You Wear?

JOURNAL

My Investment in Wholeness

_____

_____

_____

_____

_____

_____

_____

_____

_____

_____

Day 39

Thy Will Be Done

Thy kingdom come; Thy will be done in earth, as it is in heaven (Matt. 6:10).

I am going to make a statement that may be a little shocking, but it is nonetheless the truth. Jesus did not come to earth to suffer and die so that you might go to heaven. Although heaven is indeed a benefit of your relationship with Jesus, making a way for you to get there was not His primary mission when He took on the form of humanity. Jesus did not come to get you to heaven, but rather to get heaven to you.

There's an old hymn that goes like this:

When we all get to heaven,
What a day of rejoicing that will be.
When we all see Jesus
We'll sing and shout the victory.

That's a nice little song, but it implies that there is no victory this side of heaven, and that's not true. It is God's plan that you have victory in every area of your life right here and now and that you do your shouting on the earth as a testament of His goodness.

Signs and wonders are to follow those that believe in Jesus as a living testimony to the lost that He lives (Mark 16:17). I want to encourage you to set your vision on obtaining a full covenant victory in every area of your life while you are living and stop expecting it to only be available to you in the Sweet By and By.

If you believe that you will not receive an overcomer's crown until you reach the portals of glory, you are sadly mistaken. There is nothing to overcome in heaven. The crowns that are presented in heaven are earned here in the earth, so you must win your victories now. Set your sights toward total victory. God longs to present you with your crowns now so the enemy can see them clearly. From a spiritual vantage point, those crowns mark you as a member of the royal priesthood.

During this **40 Days** I encourage you to add to your prayers, "Thy will be done in me right now as it is in heaven." There is no sickness, no disease, no pain and no loss in heaven. See that for your life right now… no more pain… no more loss. Jesus came and brought heaven to you, so reach out in faith and take it.

Oh, Victory in Jesus,
My Savior forever.
He sought me and He bought me
With His redeeming Blood.
He loved me ere I knew Him
And all my love is due Him.
He plunged me to victory
Beneath the cleansing flood.

Your victory is complete. Heaven on earth is available for you now. Live in it and enjoy its benefits.

My Decree for Today

I am a victor in Jesus, and I have already conquered _____. It has no power over me, and I am whole and free. There is no weapon formed against me that can prosper because I am well immersed in the redeeming Blood of Jesus. Nothing but wholeness can find me there.

Christianity is not a life insurance policy from which one benefits only by dying.

—Unknown

Day 39

Thy Will Be Done

J O U R N A L

My Investment in Wholeness

_____

_____

_____

_____

_____

_____

_____

_____

_____

_____

_____

_____

Day 40

What's Next?

...then He sayeth to the sick of the palsy, Arise, take up thy bed and go unto thy house. And he arose and departed to his house (Matt. 9:6-7).

Today is the last day of this **40 Day** journey, and I rejoice with you over all God has done in your life. I am sure that you have received many things from Him that you will not fully realize until later. I encourage you to go back and reread your journal pages. Whenever I do that, I often see things that I missed when I recorded them in the first place. Paper is wonderful. It remembers what you have long since forgotten. I trust that journaling will become a part of your ongoing relationship with Jesus just as it is mine.

I chose today's verse to leave you with because it is so filled with power for the full manifestation of your wholeness. Jesus gave a very specific command to the man He healed of the palsy. Jesus told him to get up and do something he couldn't do before. You have taken this **40 Day** journey, believing in faith for a manifestation of health in your body, now is the time to add works to that faith.

You need to see what really happened in our scripture for today. Notice that Jesus did nothing to heal the man with the palsy while he lay on his bed. The man did not stand up healed, walk around for awhile, visit with his friends, send an e-mail to his grandmother telling her the good news and then hear Jesus say, "Arise, take up thy bed and walk."

That's not what happened at all. This man's healing didn't even begin until He believed he could do what Jesus said, and then attempted to do it. It was in his doing that the palsy totally left him and his health was restored.

What are you still unable to do? I am not suggesting that you should just randomly pick something to do as an act of your faith. You will notice in today's verse that the man with the palsy did not make his own choice about what action he should take. He simply obeyed the voice of Jesus.

That is exactly what you should do, too. Ask Jesus what He would have you to do. Right now, quietly ask the Lord what works He would have you do to add to your faith to release a manifestation of wholeness. Whatever He says, attempt to do it immediately.

Jesus might give you a seemingly bazaar instruction, but it is more rare than common that He will. He is loving and patient and isn't in the business of giving you tests which He knows you'll fail. Yes, He will definitely stretch your faith, but He rarely requires the impossible... at least not immediately. He may ask you to do something difficult, but He doesn't usually ask you to stretch your faith for the impossible at first. So, ask, listen and then immediately obey.

One last note of encouragement... your healing comes by faith, and you will keep it the same way, so stay in the Word so you can remain in faith all the days of your life. Trust the God who heals you to keep you. Stay away from people who will speak faith—destroying words into your life. Surround yourself with those who will agree with your healing and strengthen your faith.

Now take a deep breath, and rejoice over your healing. I rejoice with you. It's all over but the celebration.

Write a paragraph about the difference these **40 Days** have made in your spiritual life.

_____

_____

_____

_____

_____

_____

_____

List the answers to prayer that you have witnessed for others in this **40 Days** of prayer:

_____

_____

_____

_____

_____

_____

List the ways in which you have seen healing and divine health begin to manifest in your body:

_____

_____

_____

_____

_____

_____

_____

_____

My Decree for Today

I am whole in Jesus and will not be bound to any limitations of my natural flesh. I am calling my spirit and soul man to unite with God's Word, and I say, "Body, you must follow. You don't have a vote. You must line up to the provisions of my covenant of health. I will fulfill God's purpose for my life, and I will not be hindered by you."

Even if you're on the right path, you'll get run over if you don't get out of the way.

—Will Rogers

Day 40

What's Next?

J O U R N A L

My Investment in Wholeness

_____

_____

_____

_____

_____

_____

_____

_____

_____

_____

_____

_____

_____

Testimony

have used Freeda Bowers' **40 Day** plan many times. I am currently on my 9th **40 Days** of prayer.

God has put several people on my heart to pray for while giving Him **40 Days**, and I have witnessed many wonderful answers to prayer. God heals in so many different ways, and I have seen physical healing, financial healing and emotional healing all come as a result of my **40 Days** with Him. I have also seen healing in family situations. During one of my **40 Days**, after enduring over two months of enormous swelling that had no apparent reason detectible by MRI or X-rays, my own knee problem was cured without surgery. On the last day of one of my **40 Day** plans my friend's daughter received a good medical report, and the answers to prayer go on and on.

After experiencing such things I can't wait to start another **40 Days** with God. He is the Author and Finisher of all things, and all I have to do is show up with faith.

—LKB, Texas

Resources

For additional resources by Freeda Bowers or to contact

her to speak at your next event, please write or call:

Freeda Bowers Ministries
P.O. Box 608752
Orlando, FL 32860
For bookings & product order only,
call 1-877-409-4040.
For additional inquiries,
call 407-862-0740.

E-Mail: freeda@freedabowers.com
Web Page: http://www.freedabowers.com

R

Additional copies of **Give Me 40 Days for Healing** are available.

Give Me 40 Days

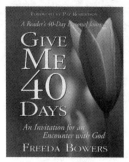

■ This beautiful hardcover book is a timeless and practical devotional to help you put everything in your life (marriage, children, finances, fears, hopes and dreams) into a daily connection with Jesus. **Give Me 40 Days** will teach and convince you why above all else … Prayer is More Important. *Hardcover book.*

Binding and Loosing

■ An illuminating teaching based upon the instructions of Jesus found in Matthew 16:19 and 18:18. There has been a great deal of confusion and controversy about what Jesus refers to in these passages. In this teaching Freeda gives a clear and concise understanding from the Scriptures of what Jesus imparts to His followers. Freeda shows how to effectively pray powerful "binding and loosing" prayers using as samples some prayers for the most common problems facing mankind today. *Booklet and two CDs in an album.*

Over My Dead Body

■ A vital message on the marriage covenant. God's will that marriage be forever is viewed through His eyes as Freeda takes you through the Scriptures teaching God's intended purpose for the marriage union, revealing how we often fall far short of the joy available to us. *Booklet.*

Generational Repentance

■ An enlightening teaching on destroying generational curses. Many families are plagued generation after generation with besetting sin and destructive addictive behaviors. Co-teaching with her personal assistant Linda Markowitz, Freeda exposes the root of generational captivity and gives the tools necessary to set the captives free. *Booklet and two CDs in an album.*

Where is Your Heart?

■ Freeda exposes one of the greatest tools of the enemy. You can be doing all of the "right" things, but with a wrong heart motive and sadly find your efforts burned as wood, hay and stubble on the Day of Judgment. The Lord looks upon our heart, and this wonderful teaching reveals the necessity of examining your own. *Booklet.*

Secrets to Prevailing Prayer

■ David prayed prayers that prevailed against enormous obstacles and is the only person recorded in the Bible to have the heart of God. What did David know that perhaps we have missed? In this insightful teaching Freeda gives five wonderful prayer keys that could become the five smooth stones you need to overcome the Goliaths in your life. *Booklet.*